EMPOWER

YOUR

HOW TO TRANSFORM YOUR **LIFE** WITH A COMPREHENSIVE **GUIDE FOR** REDUCING STRESS, INCREASING RESILIENCE, **AND** ACHIEVING BALANCE **IN YOUR** LIFE, WORK, **AND** RELATIONSHIPS

SELF-CARE

SCOTT ALLAN

Empower Your Self Care

*How to Transform Your Life with a Comprehensive Guide for **Reducing Stress, Increasing Resilience**, and **Achieving Balance in Your Life, Work, and Relationships***

More Bestselling Titles From Scott Allan

The Discipline of Masters

Do the Hard Things First

Undefeated

No Punches Pulled

Fail Big

Rejection Free

Check out the complete collection of books and training here:

www.scottallanbooks.com

Empower Your
Self-Care

*How to Transform Your Life with a Comprehensive Guide for **Reducing Stress, Increasing Resilience,** and **Achieving Balance in Your Life, Work, and Relationships***

By Scott Allan

Copyright page

CONTENTS

Introduction: Empower Your Self-care

"Be patient with yourself. Self-growth is tender; it's holy ground. There's no greater investment."

— Stephen Covey

Do you struggle with finding joy in life? Do you often feel like your life is more about doing things for others and less about your own self? Do you feel you are too busy to have time to take care of yourself and your needs? Has all this made you feel emotionally drained, especially when life throws a curveball your way?

If the above questions describe you, here is the thing:

While these feelings might have many causes, a lack of or inadequate self-care is often their primary cause. That is why you need to understand the importance of self-care, then take gradual and consistent action to integrate it into your life.

If you've ever thought, "I need to take better care of myself," you will enjoy reading this book. You will also find this book valuable because it focuses on helping you find joy, peace, and happiness by engaging in simple but highly effective self-care practices and habits.

Self-care is essential to maintaining our physical, mental, and emotional well-being, but it can be challenging to prioritize and practice self- in our busy lives. That's where this handy and practical guide comes in.

From this book, you will learn practical self-care tips and techniques you can incorporate into your daily routine and strategies to help you overcome common obstacles and challenges.

Here is a sneak peek of what you'll learn from this guide:

- **Actionable strategies to improve physical health:** You'll find really practical tips and strategies you can use to improve nutrition, exercise, sleep, and personal hygiene, which are all essential for maintaining physical health and well-being.

- **Workable stress-busting techniques and tips:** You will learn proven tactics for managing stress and emotions, including stress reduction techniques, communication skills, and mindfulness practices.

- **Relationships and you:** You will also learn viable strategies for building and maintaining healthy relationships, which can provide support and fulfillment in our lives.

- **Tips to increase productivity and balance:** We shall also discuss effective tips that'll help improve your time management and goal-setting processes, which can help us become more productive and achieve a sense of balance in our lives.

- We shall also look into practicing self-compassion and taking breaks to recharge and care for ourselves, which can improve overall well-being and happiness.

Whether you're struggling to find time for self-care or simply looking for ways to improve your overall well-being, this book has something for you.

When you're ready, let's embark on a journey of empowering your self-care because you need you the most.

Section 1:

Self-care: What it is, Why it Matters, and Everything in Between

Chapter 1: Understanding the Need for Self-Care

"When you focus on yourself and love yourself, some relationships have to go"
— Adrian Michael

According to Google Trends, the search term 'self-care' has trended upward as the number of searches for the term has doubled since 2015.

This increase in interest is due to the growing levels of anxiety and depression in society, many of which we can attribute to daily stressors and the fast pace of life facilitated by technology.

Kelsey Patel, a wellness expert, explains that self-care is part of the solution to coping with stress because it helps individuals unwind and slow down, reducing feelings of anxiety and overwhelm.

But what exactly is self-care, and why is it important?

Let's find that out.

Defining Self-Care

The World Health Organization defines self-care as *"the ability to promote health, prevent disease, maintain health, and cope with illness and disability, with or without the support of a healthcare provider."*

This definition encompasses all the actions you can take to maintain physical health, such as hygiene, nutrition, and seeking medical care, and also emotional health by managing stress and prioritizing your health and well-being.

Simply put, self-care refers to the different things and practices you deliberately engage in to maintain your physical, mental, and emotional health.

It encompasses numerous activities such as exercise, healthy eating, stress management techniques, adequate sleep, practicing self-compassion and mindfulness, and seeking professional support when necessary.

The ultimate goal of self-care is to put your well-being first and promote overall health and happiness above everything else. So, when you look after yourself, take care of your hygiene, eat well, and go after and achieve goals that bring you joy, that is self-care.

What Counts as Self-Care (and What Doesn't)

It's near impossible to describe the fundamental essence of self-care because it varies from person to person.

The underlining rule is that self-care brings you a more sustained sense of joy and fulfillment. Although we can name many examples of self-care practices that walk the narrow line between self-indulgence and health-enhancing behaviors, when it comes down to it, it is about anything that makes you feel good. That 'thing' does not have to be luxurious or cause a dent in your wallet.

Consider going for a massage at the spa or a mini vacation; they both may seem indulgent. However, if it helps relieves stress and makes you feel special and good about yourself, it counts as self-care. To your friend, that may not be as relaxing as walking barefoot on the ground and strolling in the forest. To him, that may be his idea of self-care.

One important thing to note is that self-care is a routine-centric concept more than it is about anything else. It is about caring for yourself regularly because when you do, you can successfully sustain the sense of peace and relaxation the activity brings you. When healthy, feel-good practices last a while, their effect becomes profound.

Let us look at how you stand to benefit by practicing self-care:

Why Self-Care is Critical for Your Well-Being

Self-care and well-being are critical for maintaining a healthy mind and body, reducing stress and anxiety, improving mood and self-esteem, and leading to a more fulfilling life.

Regular self-care practices like exercise, eating a nutritious diet, getting enough sleep, and engaging in activities you enjoy can help you manage daily challenges and promote a positive outlook on life. Neglecting self-care can have the opposite effect and lead to physical and mental health problems over time.

Let's dive deeper into why self-care is essential for your emotional, psychological, and physical well-being.

Reduces stress and anxiety

Self-care practices take your mind off your daily routine or even stressors in your life. When you do things you enjoy, it helps you unwind, which mitigates your stress and anxiety.

Engaging in self-care activities like yoga, meditation, or simply taking a relaxing bath can help reduce stress and anxiety levels, thus calming the mind and promoting a deeper sense of well-being.

Improves physical health

Caring for yourself also entails caring for your body—health is wealth. Self-care practices like working out, healthy eating, and getting enough sleep all do their part to improve your overall physical health, increase energy levels, and boost the immune system.

Enhances mood

Regular self-care practices can help improve your mood and combat depression, promoting a positive outlook.

For instance, practicing gratitude every morning, re-living good memories, or painting daily because it makes you happy automatically uplifts your spirits.

Boosts self-esteem

Taking care of yourself is a lot like investing in your personal well-being. It makes you feel cared for because someone—yourself—is giving you the much-needed time and attention we all want. Because of this, you will start to feel good and important; this feeling will improve your self-esteem and give you a stronger sense of self-worth.

Improves sleep quality

Many of us often seek joy in doing fun activities that often compromise our sleep.

For example, binge-watching Netflix till late at night, hanging out with friends past midnight, and excessive drinking over the weekend. While there's no harm in engaging in these activities, such things often compromise our sleep quality, which is essential for our well-being. We cannot stay sane and happy for long if we are drowsy most of the time.

When you start caring for yourself, you better understand your body's needs, which gradually helps you realize the importance of sleep, so you start sleeping better.

Moreover, engaging in other calming, self-care activities can help you feel relaxed, thus making it easier to initiate and maintain sleep at night.

Increases resilience

Many of us often break down at the littlest hint of a setback because we feel so emotionally weak. Regular self-care helps ward off those tensions by improving your emotional well-being. It resultantly builds resilience and increases your ability to cope with stress and challenges, promoting a more positive outlook on life.

Promotes better relationships

When you engage in self-care, you can manage stress better, which can often lead to improved relationships with friends, family, and romantic partners.

How reassuring does all this sound to you? Well, that's the magic of self-care. That is also why I wrote this book: to empower you with self-care habits, tips, and ideas you can use to feel great about yourself all the time. Even during hard times—and there will be hard times—the power of creating your personal self-care management system can change your life.

Throughout the rest of this book, let's find out how...

Chapter 2: The Self-Care Framework

"You can't always control what goes on outside. But you can always control what goes on inside."
—Wayne Dyer

Humans experience many regular setbacks, most of which are out of our control and often happen without our consent.

But here is the truth...

We can always control what goes on inside us. We are within our control. We can choose to make things and our own life better *always*. And for that to happen, we need to nourish ourselves first. We need to empower our self-care! That's where the self-care framework steps in.

What is the Self-Care Framework?

The self-care framework is a basic set of guidelines that create the foundation for taking better care of yourself. Just like you need a basic plan to execute any goal, you need the self-care framework to nurture and nourish yourself.

But to work on and structure the self-care framework, you need a basic understanding of the different types of self-care.

You see, self-care is an encompassing term for different ideals, habits, practices, and strategies, all guided by one principle: to make you the center of attention. That's why self-care entails different aspects of yourself and your personality.

You are a living being with emotions, a heart, a soul, a body, personal needs, different relationships, different responsibilities, interests, and hobbies, and a life to live too.

Considering all that, you must look after the different aspects of your existence and well-being.

Here are the primary components involved in self-care:

- **Physical self-care** encompasses all things and activities associated with your physical well-being. From your sleep to diet to nutrition to exercise to physical fitness to personal hygiene and medical care- physical self-care is all about taking care of your physical needs.

- **Mental and emotional self-care and health** are crucial for a happy, healthy life. This can involve taking better care of your emotions or understanding your emotional needs. It can also be about establishing effective communication with your loved ones and others or learning how to set clear and meaningful boundaries. It can also be about managing routine stress and anxiety, building your self-esteem, and attaining the confidence to live life on your terms without hurting anyone.

- **Spiritual Self-care:** Just like your body, your spirit also has some needs. It craves to be in the moment and to feel a sense of purpose in life. While spirituality may mean different things to different people, its essence lies in finding a clear direction in life. Spiritual self-care involves finding your purpose, getting clarity about things, being in the moment, and living each day more mindfully.

- **Practical Self-care:** We have a practical life that revolves around our work, goals, passion projects, and different activities that make life meaningful for us. It encompasses time management, setting the right goals, prioritizing the right things in life, taking breaks for yourself, engaging in passion projects, and creating work-life balance.

- **Social Self-care:** Human beings are social creatures; thus, we naturally crave social connections and activities. Not getting enough of those makes you socially frustrated. Social self-care is more about surrounding yourself with people who bring you joy, building and sustaining happy and meaningful relationships, and engaging in social activities that help you feel peaceful, relaxed, and joyful.

We all need all these types of self-care to feel more fulfilled, healthy, emotionally secure, fit, and well-rounded. That's how we feel our best and give our best shot to everything we do.

To do that right, you need to follow the self-care framework. Let's discuss it in a bit more detail.

How to Follow the 7-Step Self-Care Framework

Self-care is often challenging to start, especially if it's been a while since self-care was a priority in your life. If caring for yourself has felt more like a luxury at some point, this book is here to offer you all the help you need.

The self-care framework helps you slowly understand and then prioritizes your needs. An important point to note here is that the framework is a basic layout anyone can follow; it is not a set-in-stone thing. You can tweak it, change the sequence of activities and play with it to create something that suits and fits you.

To get started with self-care, here are the seven components of the self-care framework:

1. Identify your self-care needs

Identifying your self-care needs is crucial to taking care of yourself and improving your overall well-being.

Self-care encompasses taking care of both your physical and emotional health and can include elements like exercise, healthy eating, getting enough sleep, engaging in hobbies, spending time with loved ones, and managing stress.

Because everyone's self-care needs are unique, it is important to understand what works best for you, whether that's taking a long walk, reading a book, or practicing mindfulness. It is important to regularly assess your needs and make time for self-care, as this can help you feel refreshed, recharged, and better equipped to handle life's challenges.

Take a journal and write down how you define self-care and assess your most important needs. Once you understand those, put the note on your fridge, bathroom mirror, wardrobe, or anywhere else where you can see it often, thus getting gentle reminders to take care of your needs.

2. Make self-care a priority

Secondly, make self-care a non-negotiable part of your routine—like eating or sleeping. Yes, it means you must prioritize self-care and schedule it in advance.

Also, focus on setting boundaries to protect your self-care time; be mindful of your activities and daily commitments, especially those that can compromise your self-care time.

Additionally, establish a self-care routine that works for you and stick to it, even on days when you may feel too busy or stressed. Remember that self-care is not selfish; it's a necessary component that promotes your overall health and well-being. By prioritizing self-care, you can help ensure you have the energy and resources to care for yourself and others.

3. Take care of your physical health

Pay attention to your body and listen to its signals. If you feel tired, take a break and rest. If you feel pain or discomfort, seek medical attention. Regular check-ups with a doctor can also help prevent or catch health problems early.

Additionally, engaging in stress-reducing activities such as yoga, meditation, or deep breathing can help promote physical well-being and relaxation. It is also important to avoid harmful habits such as smoking, excessive alcohol consumption, and drug use.

You can improve your overall health and well-being by looking after your physical health through self-care.

4. Manage stress and emotions

Once you work on the initial steps, you must also engage in activities that bring you joy and fulfillment, such as hobbies or spending time with loved ones. Practicing self-compassion and positive self-talk can help improve your mental and emotional well-being.

Seeking professional support when needed can also make all the difference. It can include seeing a therapist, counselor, or psychologist to learn how to manage emotions, stress, and mental health concerns.

Building a strong support system and maintaining healthy relationships can also provide emotional and mental support, especially during challenging times.

NOTE: It is important to remember that seeking help is a strength, not a weakness, and that taking care of your mental and emotional health is just as important as taking care of your physical health.

5. Nurture your spiritual well-being

Spiritual self-care can also involve exploring and understanding your values, beliefs, and spirituality and finding ways to live in alignment with them.

Spiritual well-being may include prayer, meditation, yoga, journaling, or connecting with nature. It can also involve volunteering, helping others, and contributing to causes that are important to you. By engaging in spiritual self-care, you can gain a deeper sense of meaning, connection, and purpose in life, which can often contribute to a greater sense of overall well-being and happiness.

It is essential to remember that spiritual self-care is a personal and individual experience; thus, what works for one person may not work for another. Moreover, explore and experiment to find what nourishes your spirit and brings you a sense of connection and purpose.

6. Build and maintain positive relationships

Once you start falling more in love with yourself, focus on social self-care.

Start setting boundaries, taking time for yourself when necessary, and learning to communicate effectively with others. This can include saying "no" to commitments not aligned with your values or that drain your energy and spending time with people who bring positivity and support into your life.

It can also involve volunteering, joining a club or community group, or participating in activities that bring you joy and fulfillment.

By engaging in social self-care, you can build and maintain healthy relationships, gain support and connection, and contribute to a greater sense of overall well-being and happiness.

7. Take care of practical matters

Lastly, start working on practical self-care. Practical self-care can include creating and sticking to a budget, prioritizing tasks and managing time effectively, setting achievable and realistic goals, and surrounding yourself with positive and supportive people. Taking care of your physical and mental health and personal relationships can also be part of practicing practical self-care.

This guide will focus on discussing practical ideas you can use to work on all the different types of self-care, with each of these seven steps of the self-care framework explained in greater detail in the following chapters.

Empowering your self-care isn't a fortnight job. It is an ongoing task that requires constant effort and love from your end. And so, as we get started, I implore you to consider this guide a constant companion that is always there for you whenever you need to reboot your self-care routine.

Let's move forward quickly by focusing on nurturing your **physical self-care**.

Section 2:
Practical Ways to Integrate Self-Care into Your Daily Life

Chapter 3: Practicing Physical Self-Care with Powerful Self-Care Habits

"Keep taking time for yourself until you are you again." —Lalah Delia

The routine stress of daily life, years of ignoring our own care, loads of unproductive tasks, toxic relationships, and getting distracted constantly derails us from becoming our greatest selves. That's why we need to give time to ourselves until we feel and become whole again.

Physical self-care plays quite a vital role in that area. We briefly discussed what physical self-care is. Now, Let's discuss the importance of working on physical self-care to motivate you to engage more in it, along with powerful physical self-care habits that can make all the difference to your health.

Why Physical Self-care Matters

Physical self-care is important for several reasons:

Improved physical health

Engaging in physical self-care activities like regular exercise, eating a balanced diet, getting enough sleep, and managing stress can help improve physical health.

Improved physical health reduces the risk of chronic diseases, improves energy levels, and boosts overall well-being.

Enhanced mental health

Taking care of your physical health also positively impacts your mental health. Exercise, for example, can immensely reduce symptoms of anxiety and depression and improve overall mood. Eating well and getting enough sleep can also help regulate mood and reduce stress levels.

Increased self-esteem

You feel better about yourself when you take care of your physical health. For example, exercising regularly, eating well, and getting enough sleep can all help boost self-esteem and self-confidence.

Better quality of life

Physical self-care can also improve your quality of life. By feeling better physically and mentally, you can enjoy activities and experiences you might not have been able to before, leading to a more fulfilling life.

Overall, physical self-care is important because it can positively impact physical and mental health, boost self-esteem, and improve quality of life. That brings us to a very foundational question:

What habits can you work on to improve and take better care of your physical health?

How to Empower Your Nutrition

Your nutrition is arguably one of the most important aspects of your life. What you feed yourself directly impacts your health and well-being.

Taking care of your nutrition is important for numerous reasons, and a wealth of research supports this.

Disease prevention

Eating a balanced, nutritious diet can help prevent various chronic diseases.

For example, a diet high in fruits, vegetables, whole grains, and lean proteins can lower the risk of heart disease, stroke, and certain types of cancer. According to a study published in The Journal Nutrients, a healthy diet can also reduce the risk of developing type 2 diabetes.

Improved mental health

What we eat can also impact our mental health. Studies have shown that people who follow a healthy diet have a lower risk of depression and anxiety.

For example, a study published in the American Journal of Public Health found that a Mediterranean-style diet led to low depression levels.

Provides the body with necessary nutrients

According to the World Health Organization, a healthy diet can also help provide the body with the necessary nutrients, vitamins, and minerals it needs to function properly. This can increase energy levels, improve immune function, and improve overall health.

Furthermore, a systematic review published in the Journal of the Academy of Nutrition and Dietetics found that dietary interventions that focus on improving the quality of the diet (i.e., increasing fruit and vegetable intake, reducing sugar and saturated fat) can improve multiple health outcomes including blood pressure, blood lipid levels, and glycemic control.

Easy Habits to Empower Your Nutrition

Now, let's work on ways to empower your nutrition for real. Let's do so by working on easy and simple habits that can make you super fit and healthy with time.

Stop skipping meals

A major reason why we end up eating unhealthy foods is that we delay our meals, skip breakfast and even lunch at times, and then head straight for dinner after a 7 to 10-hour hiatus of not eating anything.

When we feel really hungry, we look for quick options, and that's when we start eating processed, packaged, and fast foods. The right way to go about this is not to skip meals. Instead, aim to eat small, healthy meals throughout the day to keep your metabolism running and avoid feeling too hungry.

Here's how you can build this habit:

- Set a fixed time to have your breakfast. Ensure you have your breakfast within 30 to 90 minutes of waking up.

- If you are not a big fan of having big meals, have small portions of food spaced out at 2 to 3-hour intervals.

- Set reminders for your meals and make sure to eat them timely.

You can even maintain a record of your daily meal times to keep a check on them.

Keep healthy snacks on hand

Snacking is a guilty pleasure habit for many of us. It isn't bad if we are mindful of our snacking habits. Here's a quick way to work on and improve this area of your life:

- Instead of reaching for unhealthy snacks when hunger strikes, keep healthy options, such as fresh fruit, raw vegetables, nuts, or whole-grain crackers, at hand.

- Any time you feel a hunger pang strike you, take a handful of nuts or eat a fruit.

- Have healthy snacks in your backpack, kitchen, office drawer, and other areas you regularly use or go to, so any time you feel hungry, you have something healthy to eat.

But sometimes, totally avoiding sugary snacks or potato chips is challenging. One of my favorite treats is bitter or milk chocolate, and I usually finish off my last meal of the day with some chocolate. Don't beat yourself up or try to go totally cold turkey, especially if it is something you enjoy rewarding yourself for a day of hard work. The key is to avoid swapping a healthy mean for junk.

Choose healthier cooking methods

Fried foods contribute massively to unhealthy weight gain and poor nutrition. Instead of frying food, try baking, grilling, or steaming. These methods can help you cut down on excess fat and calories.

- Set aside a day of the week for baking, grilling, or steaming to build healthy cooking rituals—meal prepping is handy here.

- Bake, grill, or steam food in big batches and freeze for later.

Read food labels

We don't truly pay attention to what we consume, which is how we keep filling our bodies with genetically modified organisms (GMOs), processed salt and sugar, chemicals, etc.

Here's a healthy habit to combat this issue.

- When shopping for groceries, read the labels to understand what you're buying.

- Look for products lower in sugar, salt, and unhealthy fats and higher in fiber, protein, and other essential nutrients.

- Know your daily requirement for different nutrients such as protein, carbs, fats, etc., and always check your products while shopping.

Eat more plant-based meals

Incorporating more plant-based meals into your diet can help you get more nutrients and reduce your risk of chronic diseases. Try to include a variety of fruits, vegetables, whole grains, and legumes in your diet.

Here's how you can gradually build this habit.

- Eat a plant every day. Even if you are having a meat-based meal, eat a vegetable or a plant-based fruit.

- Take small bites of vegetables throughout the day.

- Keep a day of the week for legume-based meals. For instance, you can have lentil soup or a smoothie.

Limit alcohol intake

Too much alcohol can lead to weight gain, poor sleep, and other negative health effects. Limit your alcohol intake to moderate levels or avoid it altogether.

Follow these tips to control your alcohol consumption.

- Assess the amount of alcohol you consume on a daily or weekly basis. For instance, you may realize you drink three glasses of wine daily; note the amount. Also, note how much alcohol you consume on different occasions.

- Next, gradually limit your consumption. If you drink three glasses, take it down to 2.5, then 2, and keep going until you have everything within a healthy range.

- Also, figure out the kind of people you meet who influence your alcohol intake. You're likely to drink more when around such people, say a friend, coworker, or sibling. Very gently, distance yourself from such influences.

As we have done with all the habits and ideas we have discussed, track and observe how this habit affects your mood and well-being.

Eat foods you enjoy

As important as it is to eat healthily and take care of what goes inside you, it is also essential to enjoy your meals and do things that add joy to your life.

While eating healthy, also eat foods you enjoy.

- If you have been following a healthy eating regimen, and feel like eating an ice cream one day, go ahead and enjoy the treat.

- If you have a sweet tooth, keep healthy, sweet items in your kitchen, pantry, and bag. For instance, you can eat more fruits, healthy granola bars, raisins, and other munchable snacks.

- Every day have at least one meal made up of foods you love. If you are a meat lover, have a meat-based meal for lunch or dinner. If you like eggs, have them in different forms at least once daily.

The idea is to make your meals more fun, enjoyable, and more about you.

Pay attention to portion sizes

Portion sizes can have a big impact on your overall nutrition. Small portions keep you full and prevent you from eating too much unnecessarily.

- Aim to fill half your plate with vegetables.

- Be mindful of portion sizes for other foods like protein and carbohydrates.

- First, take a small serving of any meal. Eat it slowly, and then sense how your tummy feels. If you feel full, don't go for another helping. If you feel the need to eat a bit more, take a few bites, see how you feel, and then only eat if you feel really hungry.

Overall, these easy habits can help improve your nutrition and lead to better health and well-being. With time, you will feel a massive improvement in how empowered you become regarding nutrition.

Now that we have covered nutrition, let's talk about other aspects of your physical well-being in the upcoming chapters.

Chapter 4: Empower Your Sleep

'Sorrow can be alleviated by good sleep, a bath, and a glass of wine.' —***Thomas Aquinas***

Sufficient and restful sleep is a crucial component of self-care. Sleep is an essential process that allows the body to rest, repair, and regenerate. Getting enough high-quality sleep makes us feel refreshed, energized, and ready to tackle the day's challenges.

On the other hand, inadequate or poor-quality sleep can lead to a range of physical and mental health problems, including weight gain, reduced immune function, mood disturbances, and cognitive impairments.

Sleep is also essential for emotional and mental well-being. Adequate sleep helps regulate emotions, manage stress, and improve cognitive function. It also supports memory consolidation and learning, which we can consider essential for personal and professional growth.

Incorporating healthy sleep habits into your self-care routine can help you feel more rested, energized, and mentally sharp. Overall, prioritizing healthy sleep is essential to self-care because it helps support physical health, mental and emotional well-being, and overall quality of life.

Some tips for improving sleep include:

- Avoiding coffee—and other caffeine rich drinks—before bedtime, and preferably after 3pm

- Avoiding alcohol before bed

- Sticking to a consistent sleep schedule

- Creating an environment that is relaxing and supports sleep in your bedroom

- Reducing exposure to screens and other stimulating activities before bedtime.

Let's focus a bit more on habits that can improve your sleep routine:

Habits to Empower Your Sleep

Adults need an average of seven to ten hours of sleep to function optimally.

You must meet your sleep requirement to sleep well and for the duration that suits you well. Here are some ideas to help you with that:

- Try to sleep for different hours at night for a couple of days during the week. For instance, sleep for 7 hours on Sunday night, 8 hours on Monday night, 9 hours on Tuesday night, and so on.

- When you wake up the next day, analyze how you feel. Observe your mood, productivity, and fitness levels daily after sleeping for X hours.

- After this analysis, you'll better figure out your optimal sleep requirement.

- What's next, then? Well, gradually build a habit of sleeping for that specific number of hours every night. For example, if you have figured out your optimal sleep duration is seven hours, but you mostly sleep for five hours every night, stretch it to seven hours by ten to 15 minutes daily.

It will take some time to get there, but the process will be well worth it in the end!

Use comfortable sleep gear

Some of us are in the habit of not paying much attention to our sleep gear. Usually, we go to bed when we are super tired without checking if the mattress or the pillow is comfortable enough.

Since we don't check if the bed, mattress, sheets, and other sleep gear are comfy enough, we keep using them until they lead to body aches and stiffness. While many of us don't consider this negligence, it is tantamount to ignoring our comfort and health.

How can you overcome the problem? Make a habit of checking your sleep gear and bedding.

- Go to bed for a little while when you are not exhausted.

- Check how the mattress, sheets, pillows, and bed make you feel. Since you are not super tired, you'll give an unbiased opinion.

- If you don't feel comfortable on that bedding or mattress, it's time to change it. If you do, keep it.

- Also, make sure you wear comfortable PJs when sleeping.

If you go through this routine daily, you'll soon have nothing but comfortable bedding.

Nap during the day

Another habit you need to work on is napping during the day. Napping energizes and makes you feel like you have more time in the day. Also, it's one of the best ways to unwind, refresh, and feel more energetic.

- Set a reminder or alarm to nap in the noon or afternoon.

- If you are not used to napping, start with 5 minutes.

- You can gradually stretch the nap time to about 20 minutes, and even 60 if you please.

However, you can skip this habit if you feel napping is not your thing. Remember, self-care is about doing what works for you. If napping—or any other self-care habit—doesn't suit you, feel free to let it go in favor of something that works well for you.

Stick to a consistent sleep schedule

Once you figure out your optimal sleep requirement, create a sleep schedule with a fixed sleep and waking up time that allows you to sleep for the optimal number of hours according to your need. Make sure you sleep and wake up at the same time every single day.

Create a relaxing bedtime routine

A healthy bedtime routine helps you unwind right before your bedtime, so you can initiate your sleep easily. Quite often, we struggle to drift to sleep because we feel stressed from working round the clock and being exhausted. That is exactly why having a relaxing bedtime routine helps you.

- Wind down with calming activities like taking a warm bath, reading a book, or listening to soft music.

- Dedicate about 15 to 60 minutes of your day to a relaxing bedtime routine and keep it about 30 minutes before your bedtime to ensure you have enough time to settle down in your bed and fall asleep.

- You can do one relaxing activity daily, set one activity for every night, or combine two to three activities.

Once you start building a healthy pre-bedtime ritual, relaxing and falling asleep will be easier.

Make your bedroom conducive to sleep

Perhaps your bedroom is not conducive to sleep. Maybe the lights are bright, or the room temperature is too warm or cold.

Keep the room cool, dark, and quiet to create a calming sleep environment.

Limit screen time before bed

We habitually use our phones and electronic devices to the point where we no longer find the usage unusual. But the truth is excessive screen time is quite harmful.

The blue rays emitted by most screens disrupt our sleep cycle and circadian rhythm (inner body rhythm that influences your sleep cycle.) Therefore, you will most likely struggle to fall asleep if you use your phone for longer hours, especially before bedtime.

Here are some practical things you can do to remedy this:

- Avoid using electronic devices for at least an hour before bedtime.

- Keep your phone and other electronic devices on silent or switch them off.

- If you feel the urge to check your phone after you get into bed, try your best to control the impulse, but be compassionate and gentle with yourself.

- You can say positive things like, 'I am in control of my urges and focusing on sleeping well.'

Gradually, you will have a better grip on your screen time and sleep better.

Avoid caffeine, nicotine, and alcohol

These substances can interfere with your sleep, so avoid them in the hours leading up to bedtime. As discussed in the previous chapter, gradually reduce your intake of these beverages after 3pm, or earlier.

Exercise regularly

Regular physical activity can help you sleep better but avoid exercising too close to bedtime.

I have dedicated an entire chapter to staying physically active, so I'll share tips on building that habit there.

Avoid naps

If you have trouble sleeping at night, avoid napping during the day.

As mentioned, everybody is different; thus, we have unique sleep requirements and routines. In case you feel napping isn't for you, avoid taking them.

Manage stress

Stress and anxiety can interfere with sleep, so practice relaxation techniques like deep breathing or meditation. Once again, this book has a chapter dedicated to stress management using effective strategies.

By incorporating these habits into your daily routine, you will sleep more soundly and wake up feeling refreshed and energized.

Chapter 5: The Art of Physical Hygiene

"You wouldn't worry so much about what others think of you if you realized how seldom they do."
— Eleanor Roosevelt

Taking care of personal hygiene is an important part of self-care. It's all about keeping your body clean and healthy, from washing your hands to brushing your teeth and everything in between.

By practicing good personal hygiene, you can prevent the spread of illnesses, feel more confident about your appearance, and promote healthy skin. Plus, let's be honest; there's nothing like feeling clean and refreshed after a shower or bath.

Practicing good hygiene habits can help prevent the spread of germs and illnesses. Regular handwashing, for example, can help reduce the risk of catching and spreading viruses like the flu or COVID-19. Maintaining a clean and hygienic environment can reduce the risk of bacterial and fungal infections.

Moreover, personal hygiene can also have social and cultural implications. For example, maintaining personal hygiene is a sign of respect and good manners in many societies. Poor hygiene can lead to social isolation, negative stereotypes, and discrimination in some societies.

Whether the plan is to get ready for the day or wind down at night, practicing good personal hygiene can help you feel refreshed and confident.

Physical Hygiene Habits and Practices

Let's dive deeper into some helpful tips for making physical hygiene a part of your self-care routine.

Establish a daily hygiene routine

A daily hygiene routine is a great way to prioritize self-care and maintain good personal hygiene. By dedicating a specific time of day to taking care of your hygiene needs, you can ensure you're keeping yourself clean and healthy. Plus, it's a great excuse to indulge in some extra pampering.

To establish a daily hygiene routine, you can opt some of these habits:

- Make sure to include hygiene habits that are important to you.

- Keep your hygiene routine consistent, even on weekends or days off.

- Try to set aside a specific time each day for your hygiene routine, such as before bed or in the morning.

- Don't rush through your hygiene routine - take the time to thoroughly clean and care for yourself.

Wash your hands

Washing your hands may sound like a small act, but it can make a big difference in keeping you and others healthy.

Using soap and warm water to wash your hands thoroughly for at least 20 seconds is the key to effective handwashing. This means lathering up and scrubbing every part of your hands, including the backs, between your fingers, and under your nails.

Washing your hands before eating or after using the bathroom and being in public places can significantly reduce your risk of catching and spreading germs. And if soap and water aren't available, don't worry; a trusty hand sanitizer with at least 60% alcohol can be a great alternative.

Take regular showers or baths

Maintaining personal hygiene also involves regular showers or baths to keep your body clean and fresh. Bathing helps remove dirt, sweat, and bacteria from your skin, thereby preventing body odor and skin infections.

The recommendation is to shower or bathe at least once a day. However, you may need to do it more often, depending on your level of physical activity and climate.

Brush and floss your teeth

Maintaining good oral hygiene is important for a healthy smile and good overall well-being. By brushing your teeth at least 2 times a day, you remove plaque and prevent cavities. On the other hand, flossing at least once a day helps remove food particles and prevent gum disease.

Remember that caring for your teeth and gums can help prevent dental problems and reduce your risk of developing other health issues like heart disease and diabetes.

Use products that work for you

Using personal hygiene products that work for you is vital to maintaining good hygiene practices. It's important to note that what works for one person may not work for another.

Therefore, when selecting products, such as soap, shampoo, toothpaste, and deodorant, choose those you consider gentle and effective for your skin type and personal preferences. For example, if you have sensitive skin, consider using fragrance-free or hypoallergenic products to avoid skin irritation or allergic reactions.

- Experiment with different brands and types of personal hygiene products to find what works best for you.

- Check the ingredients and avoid products that contain any allergens or irritants that may cause skin irritation or allergic reactions.

- Ask your healthcare provider or dermatologist for recommendations if you have any specific skin concerns or conditions.

- Remember to read and follow the instructions on the product label to ensure safe and effective use.

- Don't be afraid to try natural or homemade alternatives to traditional personal hygiene products, such as coconut oil for moisturizer or apple cider vinegar for hair rinse, if you prefer a more natural approach.

Wear clean clothes

Wearing clean clothes isn't just about looking and smelling good; it's also an essential part of personal hygiene. By wearing clean clothes, you can reduce the risk of spreading germs and bacteria that can cause illness or infections. That's why it's important to change your clothes daily and wash them regularly, especially if you've been sweating or in contact with potentially contaminated surfaces.

The next time you're getting dressed, remember that clean clothes are more than a fashion statement; they're a key part of staying healthy and hygienic.

Take care of your hair

Your hair is an important part of your overall appearance and personal hygiene. Therefore, you should keep it looking and feeling healthy by establishing a regular hair care routine that includes washing and conditioning your hair regularly to remove dirt, oil, and product buildup. You can also consider using hair masks or oils for extra nourishment and hydration.

Keeping your hair trimmed and styled can also help prevent split ends and damage. With a little extra care, you can have healthy, shiny locks that look and feel great.

Trim your nails

Regularly clean under your nails and keep them looking neat and tidy to maintain good personal hygiene. By trimming your nails straight across and filing any sharp edges, you can prevent the accumulation of germs and bacteria that can hide underneath your nails.

Also, don't forget to keep your nails clean. Bacteria and dirt can quickly build up on, and under your nails, so it's crucial to regularly clean under them to keep them looking and feeling fresh.

Stay hydrated

Staying hydrated is an important part of maintaining good personal hygiene. Drinking at least eight glasses of water daily can help keep your skin and body healthy.

Water is essential for maintaining healthy skin because it helps keep it hydrated and prevent dryness and flakiness. Drinking enough water also helps flush toxins out of the body and support healthy digestion.

Some tips you can use to make hydration a habit are:

- Carry a refillable water bottle with you throughout the day to make it easier to stay hydrated.

- If you have trouble drinking enough water, consider adding fruit slices or herbs to your water to add some flavor and make it more palatable.

- Avoid sugary drinks because they can dehydrate you and negatively impact your health.

- Remember that your body's hydration needs often vary based on various factors, including activity level and climate, so listen to your body and adjust your water intake accordingly.

- In addition to drinking water, you can also eat foods with high water content, such as fruits and vegetables, to help you stay hydrated.

Remember to drink plenty of water; it's like giving your body a big hug from the inside out!

It's amazing how just a few simple actions can improve your physical and emotional well-being. So, go ahead and give these practices a try; your mind and body will thank you for it!

Chapter 6: Boost Your Well-Being with Exercise

"A healthy outside starts from the inside."
— Robert Urich

Any discussion about self-care mustn't overlook the physical aspect of our well-being. Physical exercises are a powerful form of self-care that can significantly improve our physical and mental health and overall quality of life. Whether it's running, swimming, lifting weights, practicing yoga, or simply taking a brisk walk, there are countless ways to get moving and stay active.

Exercising regularly can help keep your weight in check, reduce the chances of getting sick, and improve your heart health. Plus, exercise can help you feel happier by boosting your mood, relieving anxiety and depression, and making you sharper mentally. Moreover, when you sleep, you'll get more rest and feel refreshed in the morning.

The key is to find an exercise program that works for you and make it a regular part of your routine. By incorporating exercise into your daily life and celebrating your achievements, you can enjoy the numerous benefits of an active and healthy lifestyle.

In this chapter, we will delve into the many benefits of exercise as a form of self-care and discuss actionable tips to help make exercise a regular part of your wellness routine.

Effective Exercise Tips and Habits

Here are some tips to help you make exercise a regular part of your daily routine:

Start small

If you're new to exercise, start with small, manageable goals and gradually increase the intensity and duration of your workouts.

- **Start with 10 minutes:** Don't jump right into a long, intense workout, especially if you haven't worked out in a long while. Begin with ten minutes of exercise and gradually increase the duration as you feel more comfortable.

- **Choose simple exercises:** Focus on exercises that don't require much equipment or preparation; this could be a brisk walk, a few sets of pushups, or some yoga poses.

- **Increase intensity over time:** As you get stronger and more comfortable with your exercise routine, gradually increase the intensity of your workouts. This could mean adding more reps, doing more advanced exercises, or increasing the pace of your workouts.

- **Be patient and kind to yourself:** It takes time to see results from exercise; be patient with yourself, and don't get discouraged if you don't see immediate changes. Remember that any exercise is better than none and remind yourself that every small step you take counts towards your overall health and fitness goals.

Make it a habit

Don't bail on yourself; you are just as important as anything else on your schedule or To-do list.

Set aside specific times during the week for exercise and treat it like any other important appointment.

Get moving throughout the day

Even if you can't fit in a full workout, try incorporating movement into your daily routine by taking the stairs, walking on your lunch break, or doing a quick stretch at your desk.

Set realistic fitness goals

Start by setting small, achievable goals you can realistically accomplish. This could be as simple as taking a 10-minute walk daily or doing a few stretches in the morning.

- **Go for a daily walk:** Starting with a short 10-minute walk each day can help you build a habit of daily exercise. Gradually increase the length and intensity of your walks as your fitness level improves.

- **Do a few stretches in the morning:** Stretching can help improve flexibility and prevent injury. Start with a few simple stretches in the morning, such as touching your toes or stretching your arms and shoulders.

- **Complete a 10-minute workout:** Many quick and effective 10-minute workouts are available online or on fitness apps. These workouts can include bodyweight exercises like push-ups and squats or cardio exercises like jumping jacks or high knees.

- **Use the stairs instead of the elevator:** Taking the stairs instead of the elevator can help you get a quick burst of exercise throughout the day. It can also help improve cardiovascular health and leg strength.

- **Try a new healthy recipe:** Eating a healthy diet is an important part of a healthy lifestyle. Try a new healthy recipe weekly, such as a vegetable stir-fry or a quinoa salad.

Remember that it's not about perfection or reaching your goals overnight; it's about making progress and establishing a healthy habit you can sustain in the long run. Keep pushing yourself and celebrate every small win along the way!

Make it a priority

Make exercise a priority in your daily schedule. If you're not a morning person, don't worry; just find a time that works for you and make it a non-negotiable part of your day. Find a time that works for you, whether that's early in the morning or after work, and stick to it.

- **Schedule your workouts:** Treat your exercise time like any other appointment by scheduling it into your calendar.

- **Wake up earlier:** If you have trouble finding time for exercise during the day, consider waking up earlier to fit it into your schedule.

- **Exercise during your lunch break:** If you have a busy schedule, consider using your lunch break as an exercise window. You can go for a walk, do some yoga or stretching, or even hit the gym if it's nearby.

- **Make it social:** Exercising with a friend or family member can help make it more enjoyable and keep you accountable. Schedule regular workout dates with a workout buddy to stay motivated.

- **Be flexible:** Life can be unpredictable, so it's important to be flexible with your exercise schedule. If you miss a workout, don't beat yourself up about it. Just make sure to get back on track as soon as possible.

Find an activity you enjoy

Choose an exercise activity you enjoy, whether running, biking, swimming, or dancing. This alone will make it easier to stick to your routine.

Here are some options for your consideration:

- **Running:** Running is a great way to improve cardiovascular health and build endurance. You can run outdoors in your neighborhood or local park or on a treadmill at the gym.

- **Biking:** Biking is a low-impact exercise that improves cardiovascular health and leg strength. You can bike outdoors on a road or trail or use a stationary bike at the gym.

- **Swimming:** Swimming is a full-body workout that is easy on the joints. It's also a great way to cool off on a hot day. You can swim laps in a pool or try water aerobics or aqua jogging.

- **Dancing:** Dancing is a fun and social way to exercise. You can take a dance class, join a dance fitness program like Zumba or Jazzercise, or dance around your living room to your favorite music.

- **Hiking:** Hiking is a great way to exercise while enjoying the outdoors. You can hike on local trails or at a nearby state park. Hiking can also provide mental health benefits, such as reducing stress and improving mood.

Incorporate it into your daily routine

Look for ways to incorporate exercise into your daily routine. For example, take the stairs instead of the elevator, walk or bike to work, or stretch while watching TV.

Instill some accountability

Exercise with friends or family members to make it more enjoyable and hold each other accountable. Join a group fitness class or sports team to meet new people and stay motivated. And hey, who knows? You might even make some new workout buddies.

Track your progress

Track your progress to stay motivated and see how far you've come. Use a fitness app or journal to record your workouts and set new goals. Remember that consistency is key when incorporating exercise into your daily routine.

Start small and gradually increase the intensity and duration of your workouts over time. With dedication and perseverance, exercise can become a regular part of your life, making it possible to enjoy its many benefits.

Find a workout buddy

Having a friend or family member to exercise with can help to make it more fun and provide added motivation. Plus, it's always nice to have someone to complain to about sore muscles afterward.

Mix it up

Variety is key to keeping exercise interesting. Try different workout types, such as yoga, weightlifting, or group fitness classes, to help prevent boredom and keep your body challenged.

Here are some options you can consider:

- **Yoga** is a great way to improve flexibility, strength, and balance. There are many types of yoga, from gentle restorative yoga to more intense power yoga. You can also try different styles, like Hatha, Vinyasa, or Bikram yoga.

- **Weightlifting** is an effective way to build strength and muscle mass. You can try using free weights, weight machines, or resistance bands. You can also target different muscle groups on different days to keep things interesting.

- **Group fitness classes** are a fun way to exercise and try new workouts. You can find many fitness classes, such as spinning, Zumba, kickboxing, and boot camp. You can also try different instructors to find a class you love.

- **Cardiovascular exercise** is important for heart health and can help you burn calories and lose weight. You can try different types of cardio, such as running, cycling, swimming, or using the elliptical machine.

- **Sports:** Playing sports is a great way to exercise while having fun. You can join a local league or play with friends. Sports like basketball, soccer, tennis, and volleyball are all great options.

Listen to music or podcasts

Listening to your favorite music or podcasts can make your workouts more enjoyable and help you stay motivated. Create a playlist or download a podcast to listen to during your workouts.

Reward yourself

Reward yourself after a workout or reaching a fitness goal. The reward could be treating yourself to a well-deserved massage, buying new workout clothes, or enjoying your favorite healthy snack.

Physical exercise is essential to self-care because it can significantly impact your overall well-being. By identifying your fitness goals, finding the right exercise program, and making exercise a regular part of your daily routine, you can enjoy the many benefits of exercise and improve your quality of life. So, don't wait any longer; get up and start moving!

Seeking medical care is another important aspect of physical care. Let's dive into it in the next chapter...

Chapter 7: The Importance of Medical Care

"It is health that is the real wealth and not pieces of gold and silver."

—Mahatma Gandhi

Even though medical care is a core part of a self-care routine, we often put it off or avoid it altogether. That's why it's important to understand the importance of regular check-ups and screenings and how to find and work with a healthcare provider that fits your needs.

Regular check-ups and screenings are crucial to maintaining overall health and detecting potential health problems early. Finding the time or motivation to make that appointment is not always easy, but it's worth it in the long run. Taking care of your physical health also supports your mental and emotional well-being.

When finding a healthcare provider, always choose someone you feel comfortable with. You want someone who takes the time to listen to your concerns and is willing to work with you to create a plan that fits your lifestyle and goals.

To find a provider that's right for you, start by asking friends and family for recommendations. You can also use online resources to research providers and read reviews from other patients.

After finding a healthcare provider you feel comfortable with, communicate openly and honestly about your health concerns and goals. Ask questions, take notes, and make sure you understand your treatment options. And don't forget to stay current on recommended screenings and vaccinations. It's a small step that can make a big difference in your health and well-being.

Remember, taking care of your physical health is an important part of self-care. By prioritizing regular check-ups and screenings and working with a healthcare provider you trust, you're investing in your long-term health and happiness.

Here are some tips that can make this a breeze for you. Let's explore some simple ways to incorporate this into your daily routine.

Pre-schedule your appointments

One way to ensure you don't postpone medical care is to schedule your appointments in advance. Doing this can help you plan around your busy schedule and prioritize your health.

- Use a planner or scheduling app to block out time for medical appointments well in advance. Doing this can help you avoid scheduling conflicts and ensure you have enough time to get the care you need.

- If you have a chronic condition or ongoing health concern, consider scheduling regular check-ups at the same time each year. This can help you stay on top of your health and catch any issues early on.

- Don't forget about preventative care like vaccinations and screenings. Schedule those in advance to ensure you don't have to worry about remembering to do it later.

- If you struggle to remember when your appointments are, consider setting reminders on your phone or computer. This can help you stay organized and on top of your health.

Set reminders

Setting reminders on your phone or a note on your calendar can help ensure you don't forget about your appointments or recommended screenings. After all, prevention is better than cure.

Keep a health journal

Tracking your symptoms, medications, and appointments in a health journal can help you stay organized and avoid missing anything important.

- Start by choosing a journal or notebook you enjoy using, whether it's a simple notebook or a more elaborate planner designed specifically for health tracking.

- Remember to write down any symptoms you experience, even if they seem minor. This can help you identify patterns or concerns you can discuss with your healthcare provider.

- Track any medications you're taking, including dosages and schedules. This can help you manage your medication regimen and ensure you don't miss any doses.

- Use your journal to track upcoming appointments and any questions or concerns you want to bring up during your visits.

- Take a few minutes each week to review your journal and make any necessary updates. This can help you stay organized and ensure you're not missing anything important.

Make it a habit

Finally, try to make medical care a regular habit. Just like you brush your teeth every day or exercise regularly, habitually prioritize your health and make time for your medical care needs.

- Create a routine for taking any necessary medications or supplements, such as taking them at the same time each day.

- Find ways to incorporate healthy habits into your daily routine, such as taking a brisk walk during your lunch break or performing stretches before bed.

- Make self-care a priority by setting boundaries and saying no to activities or commitments that interfere with your health needs.

- Reward yourself for taking care of your health; you can treat yourself to a massage or indulge in your favorite healthy meal.

- Consider finding an accountability partner or support group to help you stay on track with your medical care goals.

Bring a friend or family member to your appointments

Having someone you trust, like a friend, family member, or significant other, accompany you to your appointments can be supportive enough to ease any anxiety you may feel.

- Your companion can help you take notes, ask questions, and provide support and encouragement during the appointment.

- Ensure you discuss this with your healthcare provider beforehand to ensure it is okay to have another person present during the appointment.

- A support system can help you feel more empowered and motivated to prioritize your medical care needs. Create one made up of people who have your best interest at heart.

- Don't be afraid to ask for their opinion or input but always advocate for your health and needs.

Bring a list of questions to your appointments

Before your appointment, take some time to jot down any questions or concerns you have. This can help you make the most of your appointment time and ensure you get the necessary information.

Don't ignore symptoms

If you notice any unusual symptoms or changes in your health, don't ignore them. Make an appointment with your healthcare provider to get checked out, even if you don't think it's serious.

- Trust your instincts and listen to your body. If something feels off, it's important to take it seriously.

- Record any new or concerning symptoms, including when they started and how often they occur.

- Don't wait for symptoms to get worse before seeking medical attention. Addressing a health issue early on can often prevent it from becoming serious.

Remember that it's always better to be safe than sorry. It's better to have a doctor tell you it's nothing to worry about than to ignore something potentially life-threatening.

Use technology to your advantage

Many healthcare providers now offer telemedicine appointments that can save you time and make fitting appointments into your busy schedule easier. You can also use apps or online portals to track your medical information and communicate with your healthcare provider.

Find a support group

If you're dealing with a chronic health condition, finding a support group can provide you with emotional support and practical advice from others going through similar experiences.

Advocate for yourself

Don't hesitate to ask questions or speak up whenever you have unheard or unaddressed health concerns. Remember, you are the expert on your own body and health, and your healthcare provider should be a partner in helping you achieve your health goals.

Don't hesitate to get a second opinion

If you have concerns about a diagnosis or treatment plan, don't hesitate to seek a second opinion from another healthcare provider. It's your health, and you have the right to be an informed and active participant in your care.

Remember, taking care of your health is an essential part of self-care. By implementing these techniques and prioritizing medical care, you can help ensure you're taking care of your physical and mental well-being. After all, your health is your wealth.

Section 3: Mental and Emotional Self-Care

Introduction: Mental and Emotional Self-care

In today's fast-paced world, we are constantly under pressure to perform and succeed, which often adversely affects our mental and emotional health. It's common to feel overwhelmed and to struggle with managing our emotions and maintaining a positive mindset. But taking care of our mental and emotional health is more important than ever.

By prioritizing self-care, we can improve our mood, reduce stress, and increase our overall sense of well-being.

So, what does mental and emotional self-care involve?

Mental and emotional self-care is about incorporating various practices into our daily lives that promote overall well-being. This can include engaging in regular physical activity, eating a healthy diet, managing stress using mindfulness meditation, setting boundaries, connecting with others, and seeking professional help when necessary.

First and foremost, taking care of our physical health is a crucial aspect of mental and emotional self-care. Secondly, stress is an inevitable part of life; finding healthy ways to cope with it is the only real thing we can do about it.

Thirdly, creating boundaries is another crucial aspect of mental and emotional self-care. This aspect involves learning to say no to commitments that don't align with our values or priorities and setting aside 'me time' to engage in activities that bring us joy and relaxation.

Finally, connecting with others is vital to mental and emotional self-care. Social support can help buffer us against stress and promote deeper happiness and well-being.

Let's dive deeper into some mental and emotional health practices that will show you just how important mental health is to you. After all, taking care of your mental health is just as crucial as caring for your physical health.

Chapter 8: Stress Management & How to Revitalize Your Mind and Body

"The greatest weapon against stress is our ability to choose one thought over another." — **William James**

Stress is an inevitable part of life, and it can significantly impact our bodies and minds. Let's start with a scientific recap of what stress does.

The Science of Stress

When we experience stress, our bodies go into "fight or flight" mode, triggering the release of or a surge of hormones such as adrenaline and cortisol. This physiological response can cause varied physical symptoms, including increased heart rate, rapid breathing, and muscle tension.

Furthermore, stress can impact our mental health, leading to symptoms such as anxiety, depression, and difficulty concentrating. That's why finding ways to cope with it is crucial.

But how do you know you are stressed?

Stress can manifest in different ways for different people. Some common stress signs include physical symptoms such as headaches, muscle tension, fatigue, and difficulty sleeping and emotional symptoms such as irritability, anxiety, and feeling overwhelmed.

That's why you should pay attention to your body and mind and recognize when you may be experiencing stress, as prolonged stress can negatively affect your overall health.

Given the negative impact of stress on our well-being, it's important to find ways to reduce and manage it.

Below are the most important stress management tips and habits you can use today:

Practice relaxation techniques

To promote relaxation and reduce self-care stress, incorporate mindfulness exercises like paying attention to your breath or doing relaxing yoga poses during exercise.

The most amazing thing is that you can practice these techniques anywhere and anytime, making them a convenient and effective way to manage stress.

- **Deep breathing**: To practice deep breathing, find a quiet spot to sit or lie down and close your eyes. Inhale deeply for four counts, hold your breath for four counts, then exhale slowly for another four counts. Repeat for several minutes, focusing on your breath and relaxing your body

- **Meditation:** The easiest way to meditate is to sit comfortably in a quiet place with closed eyes.

Focus on your breath or repeat a relaxing mantra. If your mind wanders, gently recenter your attention on your breath or mantra.

- **Progressive muscle relaxation**: To relax your body, find a quiet place to sit or lie down and close your eyes. Tense and relax each muscle group, starting with your toes and working your way up to your head. Focus on the release of tension and feeling relaxation in each muscle group.

Connect with others

Connecting with others is essential to our well-being, especially during times of stress. Social support can help us cope with difficult situations and promote feelings of happiness and belonging. There are many ways to connect with others and encourage joyfulness.

Here are some ways you can incorporate social connections into your daily routine:

- Schedule regular catch-ups with friends or family, whether that's a weekly phone call or a monthly dinner date.

- Join a club or group that aligns with your interests, such as a book club, hiking group, or cooking class.

- Volunteer in your community and give back to others; you can help at a local shelter or participate in a beach clean-up drive.

- Use social media mindfully to stay connected with friends and family who live far away but balance it with in-person interactions.

- Try new things and step out of your comfort zone by attending networking events or venturing into a new hobby.

By connecting with others, we can build a strong support system and promote joyfulness in our daily lives.

Seek professional help when needed

If you've noticed that stress keeps impacting your daily life and well-being, seek immediate help because even though self-care practices can be effective ways to manage stress, they may not always be enough.

Seeking professional help from a mental health professional can provide additional support and guidance in managing stress and developing coping strategies.

Here are some steps to take if you feel like stress is impacting your life negatively:

- Reach out to a mental health professional such as a therapist, counselor, or psychologist.

- Ask for recommendations from your primary care physician, insurance provider, or trusted loved ones, friends, and family.

- Schedule an appointment with a mental health professional and be open and honest about your stressors and concerns.

- Work collaboratively with your mental health professional to develop a personalized plan for managing stress.

- Consider different treatment options, such as therapy, medication, or both.

Remember, seeking help is a sign of strength and self-awareness, not weakness. Taking steps to seek professional help is like investing in your well-being and taking control of your stress.

Journaling: Write your way to calm

Dedicating a few minutes to writing down your thoughts and feelings can be a powerful way to manage stress. Try taking a few minutes each day to write down what's on your mind or keep a gratitude journal where you write down everything in your life that makes you feel thankful.

- Set aside 10-15 minutes each day to write down what's on your mind. You can do this in a physical notebook, a digital document, or a voice memo.

- If you're unsure where to start, try using prompts such as reflecting on something positive that happened that day, writing a letter to yourself, or venting about something you feel has been bothering you.

- Remember, you do not need to worry about grammar or spelling because journaling has one chief aim: *expressing yourself to release stress and tension.*

- By making journaling a daily habit you do at the same time each day, you'll create a routine that promotes self-reflection and stress relief.

Find relaxation in hobbies

Engaging in hobbies or activities you enjoy can be a great way to manage stress.

Whether you're into painting, gardening, or playing a musical instrument, finding something you're passionate about can help reduce stress levels and improve overall well-being.

Below are some practical suggestions:

- Cooking can be a therapeutic way to reduce stress and create something delicious at the same time.

- Gardening can provide a sense of relaxation and fulfillment as you tend to and care for plants.

- Reading can be a great way to escape into a different world and take your mind off of stressors.

- Playing music can be a great way to express yourself and reduce stress.

- Volunteering for a cause you're passionate about can provide a sense of purpose and fulfillment while reducing stress levels.

Exercise regularly

You've read the chapter on the importance of exercise in self-care. Let's reemphasize:

Including exercise in your self-care routine can significantly reduce stress and improve mood. It's like adding a secret ingredient to your self-care recipe and can make all the difference. Regular exercise is a powerful stress buster and has many benefits for both physical and mental health.

Prioritize it

Taking time for yourself and engaging in activities that bring you joy, and relaxation can be one of the best ways to deal with stress.

Whether it's taking a bath, reading a book, or spending time with loved ones, self-care can help reduce overwhelming feelings and promote a more positive mindset.

Get enough sleep

It's easy to neglect the importance of getting enough sleep, especially when we have so many things on our minds. But taking care of ourselves also means taking care of our sleep.

As I mentioned in the earlier chapter on sleep empowerment, our bodies rely on restful sleep to heal and replenish. We feel drained, moody, and stressed when we don't get enough sleep.

Therefore, please commit to prioritizing your sleep by aiming for 7-8 hours of sleep per night and establishing a consistent sleep routine. By doing so, you can wake up adequately refreshed and ready to take on the day ahead.

Manage time effectively

Feeling overwhelmed by a long To-do list can contribute to feelings of stress. Poor time management can be a significant source of stress. To better manage your time, try using a planner or scheduling app to help track your tasks and deadlines. Break down large tasks into smaller, more manageable ones and prioritize what you must do first.

Take breaks

Taking breaks throughout the day is important, especially if you're feeling stressed. Take a few minutes to step away from your work or responsibilities and do something that relaxes you, like reading a book, listening to music, or taking a quick walk outside. This can help refresh your mind and reduce stress levels.

As you will learn in the next chapter, self-respect and healthy relationship boundaries are also key mental and emotional self-care elements.

Chapter 9: Boundaries and Self-Respect

"Smile, breathe, and go slowly."
—Thích Nhất Hạnh

Boundaries are an essential aspect of mental and emotional self-care. They are the guidelines you set for yourself and others to define what is and isn't acceptable behavior or treatment. Setting and respecting boundaries is critical for maintaining healthy relationships and protecting your mental and emotional well-being.

One of the primary benefits of setting boundaries is that it helps you establish your sense of self-respect. And remember, setting boundaries is like saying you value yourself enough to define and set limits on how you want others to treat you. That tells other people that you will not tolerate disrespect or mistreatment.

Like any other skill set, setting boundaries is a skill that takes practice to get good at, and sometimes people may push back or give you a hard time. But it's important to remember that you deserve respect, and your feelings matter.

Additionally, although setting boundaries might feel selfish, it's a genuine way to care for yourself and respect yourself. So be patient with yourself as you figure it out and know that every healthy boundary you set will be worth the effort.

You might wonder, "How do I begin to identify my boundaries?" Don't worry; this chapter has you covered. We will walk through everything you need to know, from figuring out your boundaries to implementing them in your self-care routine.

So, let's get started.

How to Identify and Set Personal Boundaries

Setting boundaries is vital to maintaining healthy relationships with others and ensuring your emotional and physical care.

However, before you can set boundaries, you must first identify what they are.

By following some simple steps, you can develop a better understanding of your boundaries and communicate them effectively with others:

- The first step is identifying what behaviors or actions make you uncomfortable or upset. Doing this requires reflecting on your values, needs, and feelings and may involve specific triggers such as disrespectful language or personal space invasion.

- Once you have identified these triggers, you can decide on the boundaries you want to set. Doing this may involve communicating your needs, asking others to speak to you respectfully, or asking for personal space when needed.

- When you feel uncomfortable or upset, please pay attention to your emotions because it can help you identify when someone crosses your boundaries.

- Physical sensations like tension, discomfort, or nausea can signal boundary violations, so you should not ignore such signs.

- Reflecting on your values is another important aspect. Consider what you value and what's important to you, and ensure your boundaries align with these values. This will help you to protect your values and feel more confident in enforcing your boundaries.

- Looking at past experiences where you may have felt taken advantage of or where your needs went unmet can also provide valuable insight into areas where you may need to establish clearer boundaries. These experiences can help you identify patterns and triggers that may have gone unnoticed.

- Finally, seeking feedback from trusted others can also help identify areas where you may need to set boundaries.

It's important to be firm in your boundaries and to communicate them clearly and respectfully to others while still being open to feedback and willing to adjust them as needed.

Communicate your boundaries

To communicate your boundaries effectively, be clear and direct about what you need and use "I" statements to express your emotions and needs without sounding accusatory.

Being assertive and confident while communicating your boundaries is important because it helps others understand and respect your perspective. Remember that your boundaries are valid, and you have the right to communicate them clearly and respectfully.

Be consistent

Maintaining boundaries can be challenging, especially when others have grown used to you not having boundaries or, when you have had unclear or weak boundaries. Consistency is key when it comes to maintaining boundaries.

Have a plan in place

You can't just set boundaries once and expect others to remember and respect them; having a plan for responding when someone challenges your boundaries is just as important. You can set consequences for someone crossing a boundary or use assertiveness techniques to communicate your boundaries effectively.

For instance, if someone interrupts you when speaking, you can calmly let them know you need to finish before they can speak, if they continue to interrupt.

Enlist the support of those around you

Please let your loved ones know your boundaries and ask for their help in maintaining them. This can involve clearly and respectfully communicating your boundaries and asking for support whenever needed.

For example, if you've decided to limit your social media usage, you can let your friends know you won't respond to messages or posts as frequently and ask them to respect your decision.

Be patient with yourself

Maintaining consistent boundaries takes time and patience. It's normal to feel uncomfortable or even guilty at first, but the more you practice this critical skill, the easier it will become.

Remember that setting and maintaining boundaries is a process; therefore, making mistakes along the way is totally acceptable. Be kind to yourself and celebrate your successes, no matter how small they may seem.

Do not apologize

When setting boundaries, it can be tempting to apologize—or feel guilty—for asserting your needs. However, it's important to remember that self-care is not selfish or wrong. You have the right to prioritize your well-being and set limits on what you're willing and able to tolerate from others.

Apologizing for setting boundaries can convey that your needs aren't important, thereby undermining your self-respect and self-esteem. Instead, try to reframe setting boundaries as an act of self-care and self-respect and approach it with confidence and assertiveness.

Remember that boundaries are a two-way street. Just as you have boundaries, others have theirs as well. Respect their boundaries and communicate with them in a way that honors their needs and feelings.

Chapter 10: Unlocking the Power of Communication

"She believed she could, so she did."
— R.S. Grey

Communication is a crucial part of our lives that often goes unrecognized for its impact on our general well-being.

Whether we're expressing ourselves, seeking support from others, or setting boundaries with those around us, effective communication is vital to maintaining healthy relationships and taking care of ourselves.

In this way, communication becomes a powerful tool for self-care that allows us to express ourselves more fully, understand others better, and create a more supportive and fulfilling life.

Assertive communication allows us to express our needs and opinions without feeling guilty or ashamed, leading to healthier and more fulfilling relationships.

Equally important is seeking social support through communication. Engaging in meaningful conversations with others provides a sense of connection, belonging, and validation, which can combat feelings of loneliness and isolation that can harm our mental health. So, don't underestimate the power of good communication: it can truly transform your life and improve your overall well-being.

This chapter will explore ways to use communication for self-care, including assertive communication, active listening, seeking social support, and setting healthy boundaries.

By delving into the benefits of these communication strategies and offering practical tips and techniques, my goal is to help you improve your communication skills and use them to create a more fulfilling and healthier lifestyle.

Practice active listening

Active listening is an essential aspect of effective communication. When we listen actively, we demonstrate that we value the other person's perspective and want to understand their point of view.

Here are some effective active listening guidelines you can use in daily life:

- One way to practice active listening is to repeat or paraphrase what you heard. This technique helps ensure you understand the speaker's message accurately.

- Start by saying something like, "Let me make sure I understand what you're saying..." then repeat what you heard in your own words. This helps clarify the message and shows the speaker your active engagement in the conversation.

- If you are unsure about something the speaker said or want more information, ask open-ended questions meant to encourage the speaker to elaborate on a point. For example, you might say, "Can you tell me more about that?" or "How did that make you feel?"

- Active listening also involves paying attention to nonverbal cues like body language and facial expressions; Pay attention to things like eye contact, posture, and gestures to help you understand the speaker's message more fully.

When we don't listen, we miss out on valuable information and make the other person feel like we don't care about what they have to say. Listen with intent to exercise true empathy and, give the other person your complete attention.

Be clear and concise

Use clear language to communicate effectively. Avoid confusing jargon and be concise with your language to ensure others understand your message and prevent unnecessary misunderstandings.

Adapt your language to the listener's understanding level. Doing this will help you achieve better outcomes in personal and professional settings. In other words, don't try to impress people with big words; just get your message across.

Be mindful of non-verbal communication

Non-verbal communication is a crucial component of effective communication. It can greatly influence how an audience receives and understands your message. That's why it's important to be aware of your non-verbal cues and ensure they align with what you're trying to convey. In other words, it's not just about what you say; how you say it matters too.

Your facial expressions, gestures, and posture can all communicate emotions and interest levels, whether positive or negative. By being mindful of your non-verbal communication, you can establish trust, improve comprehension, and foster a positive and effective communication experience.

- Being aware of nonverbal communication (posture, facial expressions, gestures) shows sensitivity to its impact on others. Avoiding crossing arms or slouching can convey openness and interest.

- Maintaining eye contact signals active listening, but prolonged staring can make other people uncomfortable or intimidated.

- Nodding, leaning forward, and appropriate facial expressions indicate engagement and interest in the conversation, building rapport and trust.

- Fidgeting is distracting and suggests a lack of focus or interest. Sitting still without tapping feet or playing with objects demonstrates attentiveness.

- Being aware of cultural differences in nonverbal communication is crucial. Direct eye contact, something many cultures consider respectful, can come off as confrontational or impolite in some societies.

Practice empathy

Empathy is the ability to understand and relate to another person's feelings.

It's important to note that empathy involves understanding and validating another person's feelings. This means acknowledging their emotions and letting them know that you hear and understand them. Or, as some would say, putting yourself in someone else's shoes and giving them a virtual pat on the back. When you practice empathy, you create a safe space for the other person to express themselves and feel heard.

Be open to feedback

Receiving feedback is vital to improving communication skills. Seek feedback from trusted sources to gain valuable insights into areas where you can improve. Keep an open mind and avoid taking feedback personally. Use it to enhance your communication skills and build stronger relationships.

Here are some ideas to get you started on the right path:

- Approach feedback with a growth mindset: Instead of seeing feedback as criticism, try to view it as an opportunity for growth and improvement. Adopting a growth mindset can help you receive feedback with an open and positive attitude.

- Choose people you trust to provide you with honest and constructive feedback. This can include friends, family members, mentors, or colleagues you respect and admire.

- When seeking feedback, ask specific questions to guide the conversation. For example, ask, "What did you think of my presentation?" or "What are some areas where I could improve my communication skills?"

- When receiving feedback, listen actively and be present in the conversation. Pay attention to what the other person says and ask clarifying questions. Avoid interrupting or becoming defensive because doing so can stop the conversation and keep you from learning from the feedback.

- Expressing gratitude for feedback can show the other person that you value their opinion and are open to the given suggestions. Even if the feedback is difficult to hear, thanking the person can help maintain a positive relationship and encourage them to provide feedback in the future.

Practice assertiveness

Being assertive is an important communication skill that can help you express yourself confidently while still maintaining respect for others.

Assertiveness involves communicating your needs, wants, and opinions clearly and directly without being aggressive or passive.

Seek social support

It's okay to ask for help. Seeking social support can be a powerful way to improve your communication skills. Contact trusted friends, family members, or mentors for guidance and feedback to help you grow as a communicator.

Always remember that everyone has room for improvement and seeking social support can help you achieve your goals.

Setting boundaries

Setting boundaries helps establish mutual respect and understanding. Communicating your needs and expectations clearly to others is a great way to avoid misunderstandings and conflicts. Setting boundaries also allows you to create a safe, healthy environment that fosters open and honest communication.

Adopting some of these habits will improve your communication skills and enhance your overall well-being and quality of life. Remember that taking care of yourself is not selfish; it is essential to a healthy and fulfilling life. Prioritize self-care in your communication habits and watch the positive effects ripple throughout your life.

In the next chapter, we shall focus on another very important aspect of mental and emotional health: coping with emotions.

Chapter 11: Coping with Emotions

"Self-care is never a selfish act—it is simply good stewardship of the only gift I have, the gift I was put on earth to offer to others."
— Parker Palmer

Learning to cope with and manage our emotions can help us maintain good mental health and a positive outlook on life. You can do that by practicing mindfulness.

Mindfulness involves being aware of and present in the moment without judgment. When we practice mindfulness, we can observe our emotions without feeling overwhelmed. For example, when feeling anxious, we can acknowledge the feeling without letting it control us.

Another way to cope with and manage our emotions is through exercise. Exercise can release endorphins, which are natural mood boosters. Even a simple 20-minute walk can help reduce stress and improve our mood. Exercise can also provide a sense of accomplishment that can help boost our self-esteem.

Journaling is another helpful emotional management tool. Writing down our thoughts and feelings can help us process them and gain perspective. It can also help us identify emotional and behavioral patterns, which can help us make positive changes in our lives.

Finally, seeking support from friends, family, or a mental health professional can be a key step in emotional management. Talking to someone we trust about our feelings can help us feel heard and validated. A mental health professional can provide additional support and guidance for managing difficult emotions.

How to Empower Your Emotional Management Skills

Let's discuss a few other key ideas and strategies you can use to empower your capacity to manage emotions:

Identify and acknowledge your emotions

The first step to managing your emotions is identifying and acknowledging them. Take a moment to check in with yourself and notice how you feel right now. Labeling your emotions and trying to understand their source helps you better understand yourself and your emotional reactions. For example, if you are feeling anxious, ask yourself why you are feeling that way. Are you worried about a particular event or situation?

Practice self-care

Taking care of yourself is crucial for emotional well-being. That's why you should always ensure you get enough sleep, eat well, and engage in activities that bring you joy and relaxation. This can help you manage stress and reduce the intensity of your emotions.

Exercise, meditation, and spending time with loved ones are all examples of self-care activities that can help you cope with your emotions.

Express your emotions

It is important to express your emotions in healthy and constructive ways. Bottling up your emotions can lead to more intense and overwhelming feelings. Find a safe and healthy outlet to express your emotions. You can use journaling, talk to a trusted friend, journaling, or engage in creative activities.

It is also important to express your emotions respectfully to those around you. Using "I" statements and avoiding blame can help facilitate healthy communication and prevent conflicts.

Practice relaxation techniques

When emotions become overwhelming, it can be helpful to engage in relaxation techniques that calm your mind and body.

Deep breathing exercises, progressive muscle relaxation, and mindfulness meditation are all techniques that can help reduce stress and manage intense emotions. Find a relaxation technique that works for you and practice it regularly.

Seek professional help

Are your emotions impacting your daily life and relationships? If so, consider seeking professional help.

A mental health professional can provide support, guidance, and resources that help you manage your emotions constructively. Therapy, medication, and support groups are all options that could help you manage intense emotions.

Avoid self-judgment

It is important to avoid self-judgment when experiencing intense emotions. Be kind and compassionate to yourself and recognize that emotions are a natural part of the human experience. Avoid negative self-talk and practice self-acceptance.

Practice self-compassion

One way to practice self-compassion is to be mindful of your self-talk.

It's easy to fall into negative patterns of self-criticism and self-judgment, but these thoughts can negatively impact your mental health and well-being. Instead, try to speak to yourself kindly and gently, as you would to a friend who is going through a difficult time.

- Use encouraging and supportive language that emphasizes self-care and self-compassion.

- Another way to practice self-compassion is to engage in self-care activities that promote relaxation and well-being. That could involve taking a warm bath, practicing yoga or meditation, or engaging in a creative hobby that brings you joy.

- Learning to prioritize your needs and well-being is an important aspect of self-compassion.

- Lastly, practice forgiveness and let go of past mistakes or regrets. Holding onto negative emotions can be harmful to your mental health and well-being. Instead, try to focus on the present moment and practice forgiveness towards yourself for any past mistakes or regrets.

Recognize and acknowledge your emotions

When we become more aware of our emotions, we become more in tune with ourselves and our needs. This can help us make better decisions, form healthier relationships, and improve our self-esteem.

In contrast, when we suppress or ignore our emotions, we risk experiencing negative consequences such as increased stress, anxiety, or even physical health problems. Moreover, one important aspect of managing emotions is developing healthy coping mechanisms.

- Coping mechanisms are essential tools we use to manage difficult emotions and situations.

Without them, we may resort to unhealthy behaviors that can worsen our problems.

- You can use various healthy coping mechanisms to manage your emotions, including exercise, meditation, spending time with loved ones, journaling, and seeking professional help.

- You may find that certain techniques work better for you than others, but it's important to have a range of options.

Practice mindfulness

Mindfulness entails being present, living in the moment, and observing your thoughts and emotions non-judgmentally as they come and go. This understanding can help you become more aware of your emotions and their impact on your behavior. Find a mindfulness practice that works for you, such as meditation or yoga, and practice it regularly.

Engage in physical activity

Physical activity is a great way to manage emotions. Exercise releases endorphins, which are natural mood boosters.

As mentioned, even a short walk or jog can help you feel better and manage your emotions.

Seek Support

Don't be afraid to seek support when you're struggling with emotions. Talk to a trusted friend or family member, join a support group, or consider seeing a mental health professional.

Use positive self-talk

Negative self-talk can be harmful to our mental health and well-being. When we engage in negative self-talk, we may criticize ourselves harshly or focus on our flaws and shortcomings, leading to self-doubt, anxiety, and low self-esteem.

- Instead of engaging in negative self-talk, practice positive self-talk.

- Positive self-talk involves speaking to ourselves kindly and supportively, much like we would speak to a friend experiencing a tough time.

- For example, if you notice yourself thinking, "I'm not good enough," you can challenge this thought by asking yourself, "Is this really true?" You can then replace the negative thought with a positive one, such as, "I may not be perfect, but I am capable and deserving of love and respect."

- Affirmations are positive statements that we repeat to ourselves regularly. Examples of affirmations include "I am capable of overcoming challenges," "I am worthy of love and respect," and "I am strong and resilient."

Identify triggers

Understanding your emotional triggers can help you manage your emotions constructively and in healthy ways.

Identify situations, people, or thoughts that trigger intense emotions and develop strategies to cope with them. For example, if speaking in front of a large group triggers anxiety, practice relaxation techniques beforehand to manage your emotions.

Take care of yourself

Taking care of our physical and emotional health is essential for overall well-being. Neglecting our physical and emotional needs can lead to various health issues, including fatigue, depression, anxiety, and even physical illness.

One of the most important ways to care for ourselves is by getting enough sleep, which we have discussed variously up to this point in this guidebook.

Mental and emotional self-care does not have to take up every aspect of your life. The simple and actionable daily routines we've discussed can easily help you take better care of these aspects of the self.

Because well-being is all-encompassing, let's move on to the next section where we shall focus on spiritual self-care and how to empower it in your life.

Section 4:
Spiritual Self-Care

Introduction to Spiritual Self-Care

Spiritual self-care is another vital aspect of your overall well-being that can significantly impact your mental, emotional, and physical health. Looking after and caring for our spiritual needs can help us feel more centered, calm, and connected to something greater than ourselves.

In today's fast-paced world, many of us are constantly on the go, juggling multiple responsibilities and feeling disconnected from our inner selves. This can lead to stress, anxiety, and a sense of emptiness or lack of purpose. Spiritual self-care is a way to slow down, tune into our inner selves, and cultivate a deeper sense of meaning and purpose in life.

Research has shown that engaging in spiritual practices like meditation, prayer, or spending time in nature can help reduce stress, improve emotional regulation, and enhance overall well-being. These practices can also help us develop a greater sense of compassion, empathy, and connection to others, enhancing our relationships and overall quality of life.

Additionally, spiritual self-care can provide a sense of comfort and solace during difficult times. When facing a challenging situation, experiencing loss or grief, or simply feeling overwhelmed, engaging in spiritual practices can help us feel more grounded, resilient, and hopeful.

In short, prioritizing spiritual self-care in our lives is essential to overall health and well-being. By nurturing our inner selves and cultivating a deeper sense of meaning and purpose, we can experience greater joy, fulfillment, and resilience in all areas of our lives.

This section will focus on all the habits, tips, and strategies you can use to empower your spiritual self-care, starting with the importance of finding your purpose and passionately pursuing it.

Chapter 12: Finding Purpose and Meaning

"The meaning of life is to find your gift. The purpose of life is to give it away."
— Pablo Picasso

As humans, we often find ourselves questioning the purpose and meaning of our existence. It's a natural and essential part of our individual growth and development. It is crucial for our overall well-being because it helps us feel motivated, focused, and fulfilled in our lives and gives us a reason to get up each day.

However, the self-discovery and self-exploration journey is so challenging and ongoing that it requires constant self-reflection and exploration. That's why finding purpose/meaning is so important.

How to Discover Purpose and Meaning In Life

One practical way to start finding your purpose as part of spiritual self-care is to identify your values and passions. What activities bring you joy and fulfillment? What are your core values, beliefs, and principles? Reflecting on these questions can help you identify what's most important to you and what drives you.

This self-reflection can also help you understand what you must do to align your purpose and meaning with your spiritual beliefs and practices.

These practices can help you connect with your inner self, thus allowing you to gain a deeper understanding of your values and beliefs.

Another practical tip for finding your purpose is to try new things and take risks. This can help you discover new passions and interests you may not have been aware of before.

After identifying your purpose, pursue it with intention and dedication.

If you're interested in exploring spiritual practices that can help you find the purpose and meaning of your life, here are some practical tips.

Listen to your intuition

Your intuition is that gut feeling or inner voice that guides you toward what feels right. When you pay attention to your intuition, you can tap into your inner wisdom and gain clarity on your purpose.

For example, if you're considering a job opportunity, but your intuition tells you it doesn't align with your values, it may be a sign to explore other options.

Identify your values and passions

One practical way to start finding your purpose as part of spiritual self-care is to identify your values and passions. This involves reflecting on what activities bring you joy and fulfillment and your core values, beliefs, and principles.

Here are some practical ideas you can implement:

- If you enjoy problem-solving and finding solutions, you may have a purpose related to helping others overcome challenges or positively impacting your community through innovation.

- If you have a strong desire to help others, your purpose may relate to services, such as volunteering or pursuing a career in a helping profession like healthcare or education.

- If you deeply love nature, your purpose may be in environmental activism or conservation efforts.

- If you are passionate about learning and exploring new ideas, your purpose may be sharing knowledge and educating others.

- If you have a natural talent for leadership and organization, your purpose may be related to leading and inspiring others toward a common goal or vision.

Identify your strengths

Understanding your strengths can help you find work or activities that bring you joy and align with your purpose. For example, if you're great at communicating, you may find purpose in a job that involves public speaking or teaching.

Find inspiration

Inspiration can come from many sources, such as books, podcasts, or even people in your life. For example, if you have a keen entrepreneurial sense and want to start a business, seeking successful entrepreneurs as role models can provide valuable insights and motivation.

Practice self-reflection

Self-reflection involves looking inward and examining your thoughts, feelings, and values. It can help you gain clarity and perspective on what is most important to you. For example, journaling or meditation can be great self-reflection practices that help you gain insights into your purpose.

Incorporate spiritual practices

Engaging in spiritual practices like meditation, prayer, or spending time in nature can help you find purpose and meaning. These practices can help you connect with your inner self, allowing you to understand your values and beliefs better.

Let's look at some tips that can also help you connect with a higher power and guide you toward your purpose.

- **Practice meditation regularly:** Meditating for a few minutes, Mon-Sun, can help calm your mind and connect with your inner self, providing insight into your purpose and meaning.

- **Pray with intention:** When you pray, do it with intention and ask for guidance in finding your purpose.

- **Spend time in nature:** Nature can ground us and connect us with something greater than ourselves. Take time out for a nature walk, sit by the water or under a tree, and be present in the here and now.

- **Journal your thoughts and feelings:** Writing down your thoughts and feelings can give you clarity and insight into what you consider most important. It can also help you identify patterns and beliefs that might be blocking your purpose.

Volunteer or give back

Volunteering or giving back to your community can provide a sense of purpose and fulfillment. For example, if you have a passion for animals, volunteering at a local animal shelter can help you find meaning and purpose.

Additionally:

- Volunteering at an animal shelter is a great way to connect with fellow animal lovers while making a difference in the lives of animals.

- Participating in a beach clean-up event is an excellent opportunity to connect with like-minded individuals who share a passion for preserving the environment.

- Volunteering at a food bank can help you connect with individuals as committed to addressing food insecurity in your community as you are.

- Volunteering at a community garden is an excellent way to connect with nature and fellow gardening enthusiasts.

- Joining a neighborhood watch group is an effective way to connect with your neighbors while contributing to a safer community.

Stay open-minded and flexible

Your purpose may evolve as you gain new experiences and perspectives. Staying open-minded and flexible allows you to adapt your path and goals as needed. For example, if you realize your current career doesn't align with your purpose, you may need to pivot and explore new opportunities.

Celebrate small victories

Celebrating small milestones and accomplishments can help you stay motivated and focused on your purpose. For example, if you're working towards a big goal, celebrating your small achievements as you work toward the larger goals can provide a sense of progress and momentum.

Here are some practical ideas to help you with this:

- Make a list of small goals or tasks you can accomplish easily.

- Take a moment to reflect on how each small achievement brings you closer to your larger goal or picture.

- When you reach a milestone, treat yourself to a small reward, such as a favorite treat or activity.

- Share your progress with others who can support and encourage you to keep going.

Surround yourself with positive influences

The people you surround yourself with can momentously impact your motivation and mindset.

Surrounding yourself with supportive and encouraging people can help you stay motivated and inspired on your journey to a more purposeful and meaningful life. For example, joining a support group or finding a mentor can provide you with the positive influences you need to pursue your purpose.

- **Join a support group:** Many support groups are available for various purposes, such as mental health, addiction recovery, grief support, and more. Joining a support group can be a great way to experience a sense of community, where you can share your experiences and challenges with others who can relate and provide support.

- **Find a mentor:** Look for someone who shares your interests or career path and who has achieved the goals you want to accomplish. This person can provide valuable insights and help you stay motivated and focused on your purpose.

Pursue your purpose with intention and dedication

After identifying your purpose, pursue it with intention, dedication, and zeal. This process involves setting goals and taking action to achieve your intentions.

By aligning your daily activities with your purpose, you can experience a sense of fulfillment and meaning in your life. Pursuing your purpose with intention and dedication can also help you overcome challenges and obstacles that may arise along the way.

Spiritual self-care practices can help you find purpose and meaning and lead to a more fulfilling and meaningful life. It's important to take the time to nurture our inner selves and cultivate a deeper sense of meaning and purpose.

Chapter 13: The Art of Mindfulness

"Mindfulness is a way of befriending ourselves and our experience."
— Jon Kabat-Zinn

Practicing mindfulness is an essential aspect of spiritual self-care that can bring about a wide range of benefits for your mind, body, and soul. It is the practice of paying attention to the present moment in a non-judgmental way, which can help reduce stress and increase your overall sense of well-being.

One of the primary benefits of mindfulness is that it can help you become more aware of your thoughts, feelings, and sensations in the present moment.

There are many ways to practice mindfulness. Meditation is a powerful way to practice mindfulness, which entails sitting quietly and focusing your moment-to-moment attention on a specific object or your breath.

Yoga is another popular way to practice mindfulness because it involves mindfully moving your body and focusing your moment-to-moment attention on your breath and physical sensations.

In this chapter, we'll explore the art of mindfulness and how to cultivate present-moment awareness in your daily life. We'll cover the benefits of mindfulness, how to practice mindfulness meditation, and tips for integrating mindfulness into your daily routine.

This guide will give you the tools and knowledge you need to live a more present, mindful, and fulfilling life, irrespective of whether you're new to mindfulness or just looking to deepen your practice.

Let's discuss some of the benefits of mindfulness.

Mindfulness: Understanding Its Meaning and Benefits

Mindfulness involves intentionally focusing your moment-to-moment awareness/attention on the present moment without judgment or distraction. It involves becoming aware of your thoughts, emotions, and physical sensations and learning to observe them without getting caught up in them.

Research has shown that practicing mindfulness can have far-reaching physical and mental health benefits like the following:

- It can help reduce anxiety and depression symptoms, improve sleep quality, lower blood pressure, and boost the immune system.

- Mindfulness can also enhance emotional regulation, increase resilience to stress, and improve decision-making skills.

- One of the key benefits of mindfulness is that it can help us cultivate a greater sense of awareness and connection with our inner selves.

- When we learn to observe our thoughts and emotions without judgment or distraction, we can gain insight into our behavioral patterns and learn to respond to situations with greater clarity and intention. This can help us develop deeper self-awareness, self-compassion, and empathy toward others.

Let's look at some mindfulness habits you can try out.

Start with small steps

You can easily integrate mindfulness into your daily routine without feeling overwhelmed.

Here are some practical steps you can take:

- Take a few deep breaths before getting out of bed in the morning. Doing this can help you start your day feeling calmer and more centered.

- Pause momentarily before responding to an email, text message, or phone call. Take a deep breath and focus your attentiveness on the present moment before deciding how to respond.

- Take a mindful walk during your lunch break. Focus on the physical sensations of walking, such as how it feels when your feet touch the ground or your arm movements.

- Practice mindful listening during conversations with friends, family, or coworkers.

- Practice mindful eating by savoring each bite of your food and paying attention to the flavors, textures, and smells.

- Use a mindfulness app like Headspace or Calm to guide you through a brief meditation practice.

Practice mindfulness meditation

Mindfulness meditation is a formal practice involving focusing your awareness or attention on your breath, body, or other sensations.

Here are actionable tips that will help make this practice a regular part of your daily life:

- Set aside 10-15 minutes in the morning to sit quietly and focus on your breath. This simple practice can help you start your day with a deeply-rooted sense of calm and focus.

- Set an alarm on your phone for midday or whenever you need a break, and take a few minutes to focus on your breath and clear your mind. Doing this can help you recharge and refocus for the rest of your day.

- As you prepare for sleep, take a few minutes to focus on your breath and let go of the day's anxieties and worries. This can help you relax and sleep more deeply.

- If you're new to meditation, using a guided meditation app or recording can help you become more familiar with the practice, learn it, and stay focused during your sessions. There are many options available online, such as Headspace or Insight Timer.

Practice mindfulness during daily activities

You can practice mindfulness during everyday activities such as eating, walking, or washing dishes. Pay attention to the sensory experience of the activity and try to bring your full attention to the present moment.

Here are some examples of how to practice mindfulness during everyday activities:

- **Mindful eating**: Take a moment to appreciate your food's colors, textures, and flavors. Chew slowly and savor each bite, focusing on the mouthfeel/texture and how the food feels in your stomach.

- **Mindful walking**: Take a leisurely walk and focus on your body's movement and the sensations in your feet. Notice the sights, sounds, and smells around you. Try to be fully present in the moment and let go of any distracting thoughts or worries.

- **Mindful dishwashing:** Pay attention to the water's temperature and texture and how the soap feels on your hands. Notice the sounds of the water and the dishes clinking together, try to stay focused on the task at hand, and resist the urge to let your mind wander.

Take breaks throughout the day

Taking short breaks throughout the day can help you stay grounded and present. Take a few minutes to stretch, breathe, or simply close your eyes and focus on your breath.

Create a mindfulness cue

Choose a cue, perhaps a sound or an object, as a reminder to bring your attention back to the present moment throughout the day. Whenever you hear or see your cue, take a moment to pause and focus on your breath.

Here are some guidelines to help you with this:

- Choose a sound as your cue to take a mindful breath; this sound can be your ringtone, clock chime, or anything else.

- Choose an object as your cue to practice mindfulness; for example, you choose a plant on your desk or a picture on the wall.

- Use your commute as a cue to practice mindfulness. For example, whenever you come to a stoplight or get stuck in traffic, take a few deep breaths and focus on the present moment.

- Set a reminder on your phone or computer to go off regularly throughout the day. When the reminder goes off, take a few moments to focus on your breath and bring your attention back to the present moment.

Practice self-compassion

Mindfulness involves cultivating a non-judgmental awareness of your thoughts and emotions. That's why you should practice self-compassion by being kind and gentle with yourself when difficult emotions arise.

Mindfulness practice during physical exercises

To enhance the quality of your exercise routine and cultivate mindfulness, you can focus on your breath and physical sensations while working out.

For instance, while running, you can tune in to the sensation of your feet on the ground, or while lifting weights, you can concentrate on the resistance and exertion of the movement.

By staying present and mindful as you exercise, you can improve your overall fitness experience and achieve greater relaxation and inner calm.

Here are some tips to help you practice mindfulness as part of your workout routine:

- Yoga is a great way to combine mindfulness and exercise. As you practice yoga, focus on your breath, physical sensations, and movements.

- Running: Focus on your breath and your body's physical sensations while running.

- Strength Training: During strength training exercises, focus on your body's physical sensations and resistance to the weights.

- Dancing: Dancing is a great way to incorporate mindfulness into your exercise routine. Focus on the rhythm and movement of your body, and let yourself get lost in the music.

- Walking: Walking can be a meditative and relaxing exercise. Focus on your breath and the body's physical sensations as you move.

Practice gratitude

Cultivate a sense of gratitude by reflecting on the things you are thankful for in your life.

Here are some practical ideas that have worked for me and that might work for you:

- Start a daily gratitude journal where you write down three things you are thankful for daily.

- Take time to thank the people who have positively impacted you and your life in one way or the other.

- Practice mindfulness meditation, which involves focusing your moment-to-moment attention on the present moment and observing your thoughts and emotions without judgment.

- Volunteer your time and energy to help others in need. By giving back to your community, you can gain a greater appreciation for the things in your own life.

- Practice gratitude during difficult times because it can be easy to focus on the negative aspects of your life when facing challenges or setbacks.

Developing an attitude of gratitude can redirect your attention toward the present moment and foster a heightened sense of thankfulness and happiness in your life. It can strengthen your ability to cope with obstacles and hardships with greater strength and understanding and enrich your bond with others.

Connecting with something greater is another important aspect of spiritual self-care:

Chapter 14: Connecting with Something Larger than Yourself

"The universe is not outside of you. Look inside yourself; everything that you want, you already are."
— Rumi

In our modern society, it's easy to become overwhelmed by the demands of daily life, often neglecting our spiritual well-being. However, caring for our spiritual selves is crucial for our overall health and well-being.

Spiritual self-care demands that we attend to our inner selves, nurture our souls, and connect with something greater than ourselves. By developing a sense of spirituality, we can discover tranquility, intention, and significance in our lives.

There are various ways to engage in spiritual self-care, including attending religious or spiritual services, participating in established rituals, volunteering, connecting with nature, or engaging in activities that bring a sense of purpose to our lives. Reflecting, meditating, or praying can also promote spiritual nourishment.

Engaging in group activities, attending events, joining clubs or organizations, and actively participating in the local community can all foster a sense of connection and belonging.

Recognizing the importance of building and nurturing relationships is essential for our well-being. Taking proactive steps to connect with others and build community relationships can enhance our overall well-being and help us find greater meaning and purpose in our lives.

Here are practical ideas you can use to connect with a greater purpose:

Be open to new experiences to connect with others

Being open to new experiences and opportunities is a great way to expand your horizons and meet new people. For example, if you have always been interested in hiking, consider joining a hiking group or signing up for a local hiking event. Doing this is a great way to connect with others who share your interests and make new friends.

Join a local sports league

Whether you're into basketball, soccer, or even a recreational dodgeball league, joining a sports team is a great way to meet new people and bond over a shared activity. Plus, it's a fun way to stay active and healthy.

Attend a workshop or class

Learning a new skill or hobby can be personally fulfilling and an avenue to connect with others who share your interests. Look for local workshops or classes on cooking, painting, or dancing.

Attend a meetup group

Meetup is an online platform that allows you to connect with others in your area who share similar interests. You can find meetup groups for everything from hiking and photography to book clubs and language exchanges.

Travel

Whether within your country or abroad, traveling can provide opportunities to meet new people from different cultures and backgrounds. Consider staying in hostels or participating in group tours to meet other travelers.

Attend social events

Attending social events can be a fun and exciting way to step out of your comfort zone and expand your social circle.

Here are some practical ideas you can try:

- Attending industry conferences, job fairs, or company-sponsored events can be a great way to meet people in your field or industry. These events are an excellent opportunity to learn about the latest trends and job openings or collaborate with like-minded professionals.

- These events offer a great opportunity to celebrate cultural diversity, meet new people, and explore new experiences. For example, attending a local cultural festival can expose you to new cuisines, music, and traditions while allowing you to connect with people from different backgrounds.

- Participating in volunteer events such as charity walks, beach cleanups, or community gardening projects can provide a platform for socializing while contributing to the community.

- Social gatherings such as parties, picnics, or game nights can provide a relaxed and fun environment to meet new people and strengthen existing relationships.

Reach out to others

Reaching out to others and initiating conversations can also be a powerful way to build connections.

For example, you could invite a coworker to join you for lunch or call a friend you haven't seen in a while to catch up. Simple gestures like these can strengthen existing relationships and foster new connections.

Explore your spirituality

If you're religious, consider attending services regularly or reading spiritual texts to deepen your connection with your faith.

- If you're religious, consider attending services regularly. For example, if you're a Christian, do your best to attend Sunday church services. If you're Muslim, you might attend Friday prayers at a mosque. Regular attendance can help you feel more connected to your faith community and provide a sense of structure and routine.

- If you're not religious, explore other spiritual practices that resonate with you. Meditation, for example, can help you quiet your mind and connect with a deeper sense of self.

- Consider exploring different spiritual traditions to broaden your perspective. For example, you might attend a Buddhist meditation group, learn about Native American spiritual practices, or read about different philosophical traditions.

- Seek spiritual teachers or mentors who can help guide you in your exploration. Such a mentor might be a religious leader, a meditation teacher, or a spiritual coach.

Join online communities or forums

Joining online communities or forums is a convenient way to connect with others who share your interests, even if you cannot attend in-person events.

Whether you use social media groups or specialized forums, these platforms can provide a sense of community and allow you to connect with people from different walks of life.

Here are some great ways to connect with others through forums and communities:

- **Social media groups**: Facebook, Instagram, Twitter, LinkedIn, etc., have groups for various interests, professions, and hobbies. You can join these groups and connect with like-minded individuals.

- **Specialized forums:** Websites like Reddit, Quora, and Stack Exchange have forums for discussions on specific topics. You can join these forums and connect with people who share your interests or have expertise in areas that interest you.

- **Online classes or webinars:** Many online platforms offer classes or webinars on various topics. Participating in these can provide opportunities to connect with others interested in the same topics as you.

- **Virtual events:** Because of the COVID-19 pandemic, many events have gone virtual, providing the opportunity to attend events from anywhere in the world. Virtual conferences, concerts, and other events can provide the chance to connect with others with similar interests.

Participate in group activities

Participating in group activities is another effective way to build connections.

Here are some practical ideas for your experimentation:

- Joining a book club or attending a writing workshop can be a great way to connect with others who share a love for literature and storytelling.

- Taking a cooking class or joining a foodie group can provide the opportunity to connect with others who share an interest in culinary arts and trying new foods.

- Joining a music group, such as a choir or band, can provide the opportunity to connect with others who share a love of music and performing.

- Participating in a volunteer group, such as a beach clean-up or animal shelter volunteer program, can help you connect with others who feel just as passionate about positively impacting their communities.

Practice active listening

Practicing active listening is a key way to build strong connections with others. When engaging with others, try to listen attentively and show genuine interest in what they want or have to say.

Here are some practical ways to implement this habit:

- Always make eye contact and avoid distractions when talking with someone.

- Ask questions to clarify and understand the other person's perspective and experiences.

- Refrain from interrupting or finishing the other person's sentences.

- Use non-verbal cues such as nodding or acknowledging the other person's emotions.

- Be present in the moment and give the person your full attention instead of multitasking or checking your phone.

Remember that by practicing active listening, you can understand others better and build stronger connections based on empathy and mutual respect.

Try new things and take risks

Another practical tip for finding your purpose is to try new things and take risks.

Don't be afraid to step outside your comfort zone and explore new experiences and opportunities. This can help you discover new passions and interests you may not have been aware of before. By taking risks and exploring new things, you can expand your horizons and gain new perspectives on what brings meaning to your life.

Social self-care is another important aspect of holistic self-care. Let's focus on this in the next section...

Section 5: Social Self-Care

Introduction: Social Self-care

Neglecting our social needs can severely affect our overall health and well-being. Therefore, it is essential to engage in social self-care, which involves intentional actions meant to nurture our social well-being by fostering healthy relationships, seeking support, and participating in activities that bring us joy and fulfillment.

An important aspect of social self-care is establishing and maintaining healthy relationships with family, friends, and romantic partners. When we foster healthy relationships with the people we consider important, we can receive the support and connection we need to thrive.

Effective communication, kindness, respect, and setting boundaries when necessary are all key elements to developing healthy relationships. Simultaneously, it is crucial to be aware of toxic or unhealthy relationships and take appropriate steps to manage or end them.

Moreover, seeking support is another crucial component of social self-care. Life is full of challenges and difficulties, and it is essential to seek help and support when we are struggling.

Support can come in different forms, such as trusted friends or family members, mental health professionals, or support groups. The key thing to note is that prioritizing our mental health and well-being by seeking appropriate support is crucial.

Engaging in activities that bring us joy and fulfillment is also vital to social self-care because doing things we love can help us achieve a better sense of balance and well-being. Hobbies, creative pursuits, volunteer work, and spending time with loved ones are all excellent examples of activities that bring us joy and purpose. Making time for these activities and prioritizing our needs and interests is crucial.

Let us get started by looking at how to build healthy relationships.

Chapter 15: Developing and Sustaining Positive Relationships

"The quality of your life is the quality of your relationships." —***Tony Robbins***

Healthy relationships are vital to social self-care. These relationships have a powerful impact on our overall well-being and can offer a range of benefits.

Positive relationships can create a sense of belonging, security, and comfort we need to experience positive mental and emotional health. Feeling connected to others can also help us experience positive emotions and find purpose and meaning in our lives.

One of the most significant advantages of building and maintaining healthy relationships is support. Supportive relationships can provide validation, encouragement, and motivation, which can help boost our self-esteem and confidence.

Positive relationships can also offer a sense of fulfillment and purpose because feeling valued and appreciated by those around us can inspire us to strive for our goals and be our best selves. Through interactions with others, we can gain new perspectives, develop empathy and understanding, and learn valuable life skills.

Effective communication is a critical component of healthy relationships because when we communicate effectively with others, we can express our needs and feelings clearly and respectfully.

Relationships marked by disrespect, abuse, or neglect can lead to feelings of isolation, anxiety, and depression. Such relationships can also cause low self-esteem, self-doubt, and a lack of trust in others.

Therefore, building and maintaining healthy relationships is crucial for our overall well-being. By investing time and effort in nurturing positive relationships, we can create a support system that helps us through difficult times, provides a sense of fulfillment and purpose, and enhances our mental and emotional health.

Factors Involved in Nurturing Healthy Relationships

Nurturing these relationships involves several key factors, including effective communication, kindness, respect, and setting boundaries when necessary.

When we communicate effectively, we express our thoughts and feelings clearly and respectfully. We listen attentively to others and show empathy and understanding. By doing so, we can build trust and strengthen our relationships.

Showing kindness and respect to those we care about is also important. We can do this by expressing gratitude, offering compliments, and engaging in small acts of kindness. These gestures help to strengthen our relationships and create a sense of mutual appreciation.

Trust

Trust is the foundation of healthy relationships. It requires honesty, dependability, and reliability. Trust is often something we build over time through consistent behavior and communication.

Shared experiences

Shared experiences can help strengthen our relationships and create a sense of shared connection. These experiences can involve participating in activities together, sharing hobbies or interests, or spending quality time together.

Forgiveness

Forgiveness is essential for repairing and maintaining healthy relationships. It involves letting go of grudges and resentments and the willingness to work through conflicts and disagreements constructively and respectfully.

Setting Boundaries in Relationships

Setting boundaries is another crucial aspect of building and maintaining healthy relationships.

Boundaries help us communicate our needs, values, and expectations and help others understand and learn more about behaviors and things we consider acceptable and unacceptable. When we set boundaries, we can create a sense of safety and security in our relationships.

Here are some practical ideas you can use to set boundaries in your relationships:

- ✓ Let a friend know you are uncomfortable discussing certain topics or hearing negative comments about certain people or groups.

- ✓ Tell a coworker you are unavailable to work on weekends or after-hours, as you need time for personal activities or rest.

- ✓ Set limits on social media usage or screen time to maintain a healthy work-life balance.

- ✓ Communicate with family members about the need for personal space or alone time and establish boundaries around privacy or personal belongings

- ✓ Be clear with a romantic partner about your expectations for the relationship, such as exclusivity or the relationship's pace, and communicate openly about any concerns or issues that arise

It is also important to be aware of toxic or unhealthy relationships and seek support in managing or ending them if necessary.

Managing Toxic Relationships

Toxic relationships can be emotionally draining and can negatively impact our mental health. If we find ourselves in a toxic or abusive relationship, it's important to seek support from a trusted friend, family member, or mental health professional.

Importance of positive relationships

Positive relationships are essential for our well-being because humans are social creatures who need connection and interaction. Positive relationships can give us a sense of belonging, support, and fulfillment and help us cope with life's challenges.

Other benefits of positive relationships include:

Emotional support

Healthy and thriving relationships can provide emotional support during difficult times. When we have people who care about us and are willing to listen and offer support, we feel less alone and capable of dealing with challenges.

For example, if we're going through a breakup, having supportive friends or family members who offer a listening ear or a shoulder to cry on can help us feel less isolated and more supported.

Improved health

Meaningful and positive relationships lead to better physical and mental health outcomes.

Studies have found that people with strong social support networks are less likely to experience depression, anxiety, and other mental health issues. They also have lower rates of chronic illnesses like heart disease and cancer.

For example, older adults who have formed strong relationships with friends and family members are less likely to experience depression and have a lower risk of dementia.

Greater happiness

Positive relationships can bring us joy and happiness. When we have people in our lives who we enjoy spending time with, we feel happier and more fulfilled. For example, spending time with a close friend or family member doing something mutually enjoyable can be a source of happiness and contentment.

Personal growth

Positive relationships can help us grow as individuals. When we surround ourselves with people who inspire us and challenge us to be our best selves, we can learn new skills, gain new perspectives, and become more confident. For example, having a mentor who believes in us and pushes us to reach our potential can help us grow and develop in our careers.

Effective communication

Communication is essential in any relationship, and effective communication is key to building and maintaining healthy relationships.

As we have already discussed, effective communication involves active listening, expressing yourself clearly, and being open and honest. Being in healthy relationships improves your communication skills because you gradually learn to speak effectively and listen keenly.

Conflict resolution

Conflict is a natural part of any relationship, and learning healthy ways to resolve conflicts is essential to building and maintaining healthy relationships. This involves listening to each other's perspectives, seeking common ground, and finding solutions everyone considers workable.

As you foster healthy, happy relationships, you improve at conflict resolution, which also helps in your professional relationships.

Let us now focus on how to build such thriving relationships in life.

Chapter 16: The Power of a Helping Hand

"Sometimes the bravest and most important thing you can do is just show up."
—Brené Brown

Life is full of ups and downs, and at some point, we all face challenges and difficulties that can take a toll on our mental and emotional well-being. It could be a personal problem, a difficult phase, or an unexpected event that leaves us feeling overwhelmed and helpless. During such times, seeking support from others can be a crucial step toward healing and recovery.

Social self-care is an important aspect of our overall well-being that involves managing and taking care of our social relationships and connections. It plays a significant role in our ability to cope with stress and challenges, and seeking support is a fundamental aspect of social self-care.

Talking to a trusted friend or family member can provide a much-needed outlet to share our feelings and emotions. This can help us gain a new perspective and receive the emotional support we need.

In some cases, seeking support may require professional intervention. A therapist or counselor can provide a safe, non-judgmental space to explore our feelings and emotions.

Support groups bring together people facing similar challenges or experiences, providing a sense of community and belonging. You can find support groups for various issues, such as addiction recovery, grief and loss, and chronic illness.

It is important to remember that seeking support is not a sign of weakness but a brave step toward taking care of ourselves. Reaching out to others for help is like taking responsibility for our well-being and showing ourselves the care and compassion we deserve.

The Decision to Seek Support

The decision to seek support can be difficult for some people, especially those who value self-reliance or fear vulnerability. However, seeking support is bravely not a weakness.

It is important to remember that seeking support is a part of self-care and an act of self-love. When we reach out to others for help, we take responsibility for our well-being and show ourselves the care and compassion we deserve.

Use the following practical ideas to seek healthy support from the people in your life:

Identify the type of support you need

Before seeking support, identify the type of support you need.

Whether it's emotional support, practical support, or informational support, understanding what you require can help you narrow down your search for the appropriate support.

Reach out to friends and family

Friends and family can be great sources of support during challenging times. Sharing your thoughts and feelings with them can provide comfort and encouragement. For example, if you're struggling with a difficult decision, you could seek advice from a trusted family member or friend.

Ideally, you want to seek support from:

- A trusted friend or family member who has been through a similar experience because such a person can provide empathy and understanding, making it easier to open up and feel heard.

- Sometimes talking to someone not directly involved in the situation can provide an objective viewpoint that helps us see things differently.

- Sharing our feelings with someone we trust can also provide a sense of validation and support, making us feel less alone in our struggles.

Join a support group

Support groups offer a safe and non-judgmental space for individuals to connect and share their experiences. Whether it's a support group for addiction recovery, grief, or mental health, being part of a community that understands your struggles can provide a sense of belonging and support.

Here are some examples of support groups:

- **Addiction recovery support groups:** Addiction support groups, such as Alcoholics Anonymous (AA) or Narcotics Anonymous (NA), provide a safe and supportive environment for individuals struggling with addiction. These groups offer a non-judgmental space to share experiences and connect with others who understand the challenges of addiction.

- **Grief and loss support groups:** Grief and loss support groups provide a safe and supportive space for individuals who have lost a loved one. These groups offer emotional support and practical guidance on coping with the grieving process.

- **Chronic illness support groups:** Chronic illness support groups provide a space for individuals with chronic illnesses, such as diabetes, arthritis, or multiple sclerosis, to connect with others facing similar challenges. These groups offer emotional support, practical advice, and a sense of community.

Consider therapy or counseling

Therapy or counseling can offer a structured, confidential space to work through personal challenges. A licensed mental health professional can provide guidance and tools to cope with difficult emotions or situations.

For example, if you're experiencing anxiety or depression symptoms, seeking therapy can help you develop coping mechanisms and strategies to manage those symptoms.

Here are some examples of how a therapist can help:

- Someone struggling with anxiety may work with a therapist to identify triggers that worsen their symptoms and develop coping strategies to manage their daily anxiety.

- Someone experiencing depression may work with a therapist to explore the root causes of their depression and develop strategies to manage their symptoms, such as practicing self-care, setting goals, and improving communication skills.

- Someone dealing with trauma may work with a therapist to process their emotions and develop strategies to cope with their experiences. Therapists can use various techniques, such as cognitive-behavioral therapy, EMDR (Eye Movement Desensitization and Reprocessing), and exposure therapy, to help individuals overcome their trauma.

- Someone facing relationship problems may work with a therapist to improve communication and conflict resolution skills, work through unresolved issues, and develop a healthier, more fulfilling relationship.

Use online resources

Various online resources are available for support, including support forums, apps, and websites.

Here are some examples:

- **Support forums:** Online forums provide a space for people to connect with others who have gone through similar experiences or challenges. We now have forums for any topic you can imagine, including forums on topics like mental health, chronic illness, and addiction recovery. Some popular forums include Psych Central, 7 Cups, and HealthfulChat.

- **Apps:** We now have many apps that provide mental health support and resources. BetterHelp and Talkspace are online therapy platforms that allow you to connect with a licensed therapist from your smartphone or computer. The Calm app provides meditation and relaxation exercises to reduce stress and anxiety.

- **Websites:** Many websites provide resources and information for people struggling with specific issues. For example, if you're struggling with substance abuse, websites such as Narcotics Anonymous or Alcoholics Anonymous can provide resources and support.

These online resources can be valuable additions to other support forms, such as therapy or support groups. However, it's important to remember that online resources are not a substitute for professional help if you are experiencing a mental health crisis.

Connect with local organizations

Many local organizations offer support and resources for various challenges, including mental health, addiction, and grief. For example, if you're experiencing grief after losing a loved one, you could connect with a local hospice organization that offers grief support groups.

Here are some ideas you can explore as you seek help from local or community-based organizations:

- Mental health clinics and organizations such as the National Alliance on Mental Illness (NAMI) offer support groups and resources for individuals and families affected by mental illness.

- Community centers and non-profits such as the YMCA or Boys and Girls Clubs may offer programs and support groups for children and teenagers struggling with developmental issues, bullying, or family problems.

- Addiction recovery centers and organizations such as SMART Recovery or Celebrate Recovery offer resources and support for individuals struggling with addiction.

- Hospitals and healthcare providers may support groups and offer resources for individuals and families struggling with chronic illnesses such as cancer, diabetes, or multiple sclerosis.

- Domestic violence shelters and organizations such as the National Domestic Violence Hotline offer resources and support for individuals experiencing domestic violence or abuse.

- Religious or spiritual organizations may offer support groups and counseling for individuals experiencing challenges such as grief or relationship problems.

As part of social self-care, you also have to engage in activities that bring you happiness or joy:

Chapter 17: Engaging in Joyful Activities

"Find ecstasy in life; the mere sense of living is joy enough."

— Emily Dickinson

Engaging in activities that make you happy and joyous is a core aspect of maintaining good mental health and overall well-being.

When we spend time doing things we enjoy that bring us a sense of fulfillment, we are likelier to experience positive emotions, reduce stress levels, and improve our overall quality of life. Whether we're pursuing a hobby, volunteering, or spending time with loved ones, engaging in activities that bring us joy is a necessary part of self-care.

Hobbies and creative pursuits can provide a sense of purpose and fulfillment, allowing us to express ourselves in new and meaningful ways. However, it can be easy to overlook these activities due to our busy lives. That's why making time and prioritizing our needs and interests is important. After all, engaging in activities that bring us joy can create a sense of balance in our lives and improve our overall well-being.

The Benefits of Following Your Bliss

Engaging in activities that bring us joy can numerously benefit our overall well-being. Here are some of the key benefits:

Reduced stress

Doing things we enjoy can help us relax and unwind, thus reducing stress levels and improving our mood.

Improved mental health

Participating in enjoyable activities can also positively impact our mental health. It can boost our self-esteem, provide a sense of purpose, and help us cope with challenges.

Increased social connection

Engaging in activities we enjoy can also help us to connect with others who share our interests. Doing this can provide a sense of community and belonging, which is important for our emotional well-being.

Enhanced creativity

Pursuing creative activities can also stimulate our minds and encourage us to think outside the box, leading to pursue new ideas and perspectives that can instrumentally benefit our personal and professional lives.

How to Follow Your Bliss

Here are some practical steps you can take to find more joy in the things you do:

Find activities you enjoy

Sometimes, it can be tricky to determine what you truly and genuinely enjoy. That's when reflecting on your past hobbies comes in handy.

Think back to past activities or hobbies that have brought you joy. Consider what made those activities enjoyable and if there are ways to incorporate similar elements into your current routine.

Here are some examples of how to incorporate enjoyable elements into your current routine:

- If you used to love playing a musical instrument, but haven't played in a while, consider joining a community band or orchestra to play with others and get back into the groove.

- If you enjoyed cooking in the past but find it challenging to cook for yourself now, try joining a cooking class or finding a cooking partner with whom to share meals.

- If you used to enjoy reading but now struggle to make time for it, try setting aside a specific time each day for reading, such as before bed or during lunch breaks.

- If you have always loved playing team sports but don't have the time or energy for it now, consider joining a recreational league or finding a casual pickup game with friends.

- If you used to enjoy creative writing, but haven't written in a while, try joining a writing group or taking a class to get back into the habit of writing regularly.

Try something new

Don't be afraid to try new activities or hobbies you've never tried because doing so can help you discover new interests and passions that bring you joy.

Here are some ideas to inspire you:

- **Art therapy:** Engaging in art activities like drawing, painting, or sculpting can be a great way to express yourself creatively and release stress.

- **Yoga or meditation:** Practicing yoga or meditation can help you connect with your body and mind, reduce stress and anxiety, and improve your overall well-being.

- **Cooking or baking:** Preparing and enjoying a delicious meal or baked goods can be a rewarding and enjoyable experience that provides a sense of accomplishment.

- **Dancing or movement classes:** Taking a dance class or other movement-based activities like

Zumba, Pilates, or Tai Chi can be a fun and engaging way to stay active while reducing stress.

- **Learning a new skill:** Taking up a new skill or hobby, like learning a new language, playing an instrument, or gardening, can provide a sense of accomplishment and boost your confidence.

Schedule time for enjoyment

Prioritize and schedule activities that bring you joy, just as you would schedule time for other commitments. That way, you'll have time for what matters.

Combine enjoyment with other activities

Try to combine enjoyable activities with other daily routines or responsibilities, such as listening to music while exercising or incorporating a creative hobby into your work routine.

Try new things

It's easy to get stuck in a rut doing the same things repeatedly. Challenge yourself to try something new: a hobby, sport, or creative pursuit. You never know what you might enjoy or what might stick until you give it a chance.

Make time for fun

It's important to prioritize our happiness and well-being.

Schedule time in your calendar or T-do list for activities that bring you joy and stick to it.

Surround yourself with supportive people

Having people in our lives who support and encourage our interests can make a big difference.

Consider joining a club or group centered around your hobby or interest or invite a friend to join you in trying something new.

Don't be afraid to mix things up

Even if you have a favorite activity, mixing things up can help keep things fresh and exciting.

Here are some examples of how to mix things up and keep activities fresh:

- If you enjoy reading, try a new genre or author you haven't read before.

- If you like cooking, experiment with new recipes or cook a cuisine you haven't tried before.

- If you enjoy exercising, switch up your routine by trying a new type of workout or adding in some new exercises.

- If you like watching movies, try a new genre or a classic film you haven't seen before.

- If you enjoy art, try a new medium or style, such as watercolors or abstract art.

- If you like traveling, explore a new destination or try a new mode of transportation, such as taking a train instead of a plane.

- If you enjoy music, listen to a new genre or artist you haven't listened to, or attend the concert of a musician you haven't seen before.

Celebrate small victories

Celebrate your progress in your hobbies and interests, even the small ones. Each step forward is worth acknowledging and can motivate you to continue pursuing activities that bring you joy.

Make it a habit

Schedule a regular time for enjoyable activities and treat them as non-negotiables. Whether you do it once a week or once a month, make it a priority to engage in activities that bring you joy.

Get creative

Look for ways to incorporate enjoyable activities into your daily routine. For example, if you love reading, set aside time to read for 30 minutes each night before bed.

Join a group or community

Joining a group or community of people who share your interests can be a great way to find new enjoyable activities and make new friends. Look for local clubs, organizations, or Meetup groups that align with your interests.

Set goals

Engaging in enjoyable activities is an important part of self-care, and setting goals for these activities can help you stay motivated and focused.

Here are examples of how setting goals can enhance your enjoyment of these activities:

- **Running:** If you enjoy running, setting a goal to complete a 5K or a half marathon can give you something to work towards and keep you motivated during your training. You could also set goals for your running pace, distance, or frequency of runs.

- **Painting:** If you enjoy painting, setting a goal to complete a certain number of paintings within a certain time frame can help you stay motivated and focused. You could also set goals for improving your technique or experimenting with new styles or mediums.

- **Reading:** If you enjoy reading, setting a goal to read a certain number of books within a certain time frame can help you stay on track and motivated. You could also set goals for reading books in new genres or by new authors.

- **Cooking:** If you enjoy cooking, setting a goal to try out a certain number of new recipes within a certain time frame can help you stay motivated and inspired in the kitchen. You could also set goals for mastering new techniques or cuisines.

- **Traveling:** If you enjoy traveling, setting a goal to visit a certain number of new places within a certain time frame can help you plan and prioritize your trips. You could also set goals for experiencing new cultures, trying new foods, or learning new languages.

Setting goals for enjoyable activities can help you make the most of your leisure time and enhance your overall well-being.

Let's now focus on another key aspect of empowering your self-care: Practical self-care

Section 6:

Practical Self-Care

Introduction: Practical Self-care

"Nourishing yourself in a way that helps you blossom in the direction you want to go is attainable, and you are worth the effort."— **Deborah Day**

Practical self-care is essential for maintaining our physical, mental, and emotional well-being in today's busy and often stressful lives. It involves intentionally setting aside time and resources to care for ourselves in ways that promote balance, resilience, and overall health.

The importance of practical self-care is not something we could ever overstate because it helps us manage stress and prevent burnout, which are increasingly common challenges in today's fast-paced society.

When we prioritize self-care, we often feel better equipped to handle the demands of work, relationships, and other responsibilities and to maintain a sense of balance and well-being in our lives.

Now, how is implementing practical self-care in our daily lives important?

First, practical self-care helps us develop healthy habits that often promote long-term health and well-being.

For example, when we make self-care a part of our daily routine, we are more likely to stick to it over time and reap the benefits of improved physical, mental, and emotional health.

Secondly, practical self-care can help us manage stress and prevent burnout in our daily lives. This can equip us to manage work or personal relationship demands and other responsibilities and maintain a greater sense of balance and well-being in our general lives.

Third, implementing practical self-care in our daily lives can help us prioritize our time and resources, which can help us manage our time and resources and to live a more balanced and fulfilling life.

Also, practicing self-care can improve our physical health, boost our immune system, and reduce the risk of developing chronic diseases. It can also enhance our mental and emotional health, helping us to manage anxiety, depression, and other mental health challenges and promoting a sense of resilience and emotional well-being.

Let's focus on some worth-knowing facets of practical self-care, and some of the things and habits you can adopt to empower this part of your self-care routine.

Chapter 18: Strategies for Effective Time Management

"Time is a created thing. To say 'I don't have time,' is like saying, 'I don't want to.'"

— Lao Tzu

Time management is an important aspect of practical self-care. By managing our time effectively, we can prioritize our tasks and ensure our schedules have enough time for self-care activities. Doing this helps us better manage our stress levels, prevent burnout, and maintain a greater sense of balance and well-being in our lives.

To manage our time effectively, we can start by creating a schedule or a to-do list that outlines our tasks for the day or week. We can prioritize our tasks based on their importance and urgency and allocate time for self-care activities such as exercise, meditation, or spending time with loved ones. Setting realistic goals and deadlines and avoiding overcommitting or taking on too much at once is also important.

Another important aspect of time management in practical self-care is learning to say no. We can't always accommodate every request or invitation that comes our way, and it's important to recognize our limits and prioritize our needs. By saying no to certain requests or activities, we can free up time for self-care and ensure we are not overloading ourselves with too many responsibilities.

Overall, effective time management is crucial for practicing practical self-care. By prioritizing our time and making self-care a priority, we can improve our overall well-being, manage stress and prevent burnout, and live a more balanced and fulfilling life.

Let's focus on some key habits and strategies that will help you become a better, more effective time manager:

Set priorities

Setting priorities is one of the most underrated, effective time management strategies.

The process involves identifying the most important tasks or activities and allocating time to them first. This helps ensure you remain focused on the essential tasks relevant to your goals.

Here are some examples of how to set priorities to manage time effectively:

- **Make a to-do list:** Create a list of all the tasks you need to complete and categorize them depending on their importance and urgency. Doing this will help you stay organized and focused on the tasks you need to complete first.

- **Use the pareto principle also known as the 80/20 rule:** This rule is also called the Pareto principle. According to this principle, 80% of your results can be directly linked to just 20% of your efforts. On the other hand, only 20 percent of results come from up to 80% of the efforts! Identify the tasks with the most significance on your goals and focus on those first.

- **Avoid multitasking:** Trying to do too many things at once can be overwhelming and counterproductive. Instead, focus on one task at a time and give it your full attention before moving on to the next.

- **Delegate tasks:** If you have tasks that someone else can do competently well, delegate them. Delegating helps free up your time to focus on the tasks that require your expertise and attention.

- **Schedule time for important tasks:** Block out time in your schedule for the most important tasks. This will help you prioritize them and ensure you have dedicated time to work on them.

- **Learn to say no:** If someone asks you to do something that is not a priority or does not align with your goals, it's okay to say no. Saying no will help you avoid taking on too many tasks and ensure you have time for the things that matter most.

Create a schedule

Creating a schedule helps organize your time and ensures you have enough time for work and self-care activities. A schedule can also help you to stay on track and avoid procrastination.

Here are some helpful scheduling ideas:

- Use a planner or digital calendar to schedule your time. Make sure you block off time for both work-related tasks and self-care activities.

- Break down large tasks into smaller, more manageable ones and assign them specific time slots in your schedule.

- Set reminders or alerts to help you stay on track and avoid getting sidetracked by distractions.

- Be flexible with your schedule and allow for unexpected changes or interruptions. Leave some wiggle room in your schedule to accommodate unforeseen events or emergencies.

- Review and adjust your schedule regularly to ensure you're on track with your goals and priorities.

Use time blocking

This simply entails scheduling specific time pockets for specific tasks or activities. This technique increases focus and productivity and ensures proper time allocation to work and self-care activities.

Learn to say no

Saying no to non-essential tasks or activities can help you avoid overcommitting yourself, thus ensuring you have enough time for self-care activities.

Yeah, I know it can be quite tough to say no to someone, especially someone close to you or one you see as an authority figure. Also, if you are in the habit of being a 'yes man' to everyone, you will struggle with saying no to anyone. But, it is important to master this talent.

Nobody in the world cares about you as much as you do. That's how life is. People will mostly be there for you as per their ease and preference. If you have a habit of saying yes to any favor someone asks of you, there's a high chance that you will get hurt when someone else does not meet your expectations.

Moreover, being a people pleaser distracts you from your important tasks and priorities, leaving hardly any time to work on your tasks.

All this is to say: learning to say 'no' is something you need to train for before you can truly master it, but when you do, it can be very impactful.

Here are some practical ideas you can use to start becoming better at saying no to things that don't align with what's good for you or your higher self:

- Start with realizing that you need 'you' the most.

- Tell yourself day in and day out that you deserve your attention, care, and love the most.

- Don't rush to say 'yes' whenever someone asks you for a favor. Instead, take a moment to consider the task, the required effort, your priorities, and personal preferences.

- If you have the time and energy to tend to someone else's needs and tasks, agree to help, but only if you can do it comfortably.

- If you have something more pressing you need to work on for yourself, politely and firmly tell the other person of your preoccupation. It will sting the first time, and you may have to face a bit of bitterness from the other person, but once you gulp down that bitterness, it will be all okay.

Use technology tools

We now have several technology tools that can help improve time management; key examples include scheduling apps, productivity apps, and task management tools.

Here are some ideas to get you thinking in the right direction:

- Notion is a great app that helps you organize and manage your tasks.

- To find the motivation to complete your tasks, try Forest.

- Spark is another great app that helps you manage your emails efficiently, so you avoid distractions and focus better on your tasks.

Remember one thing: downloading new apps isn't enough. It is important that you utilize the apps you download and that you do so effectively.

Try out any one app you feel might be fruitful for you, and stick to it for a couple of weeks. Once you build the habit of using it regularly, try out another app.

Take breaks

Taking breaks is important for both productivity and self-care. Breaks can help increase focus, reduce stress, and prevent burnout. Be sure to take regular breaks throughout the day, even if they are short.

Here are some actionable ideas of how you can do that:

- After working for 2 to 3 hours, take a 10 to 20-minute break or even an hour-long one if you have the time.

- When doing a task, tune into your body and exhaustion levels every 15 minutes. The instant you feel exhaustion kicking in, take a short break.

- During your break, do anything that calms you down. You could take a quick stroll, drink something, watch reels on Instagram and Facebook, or do anything that relaxes you.

Use time management techniques

You can use one or several available time management techniques, such as the Pomodoro Technique, to increase productivity and reduce stress. Experiment with different techniques to find what works best for you.

Here are some well-known, effective time management approaches:

- **The Pomodoro** Technique involves breaking work into intervals of 25 minutes, followed by a short break. Doing this can help increase focus and prevent burnout.

- **Time blocking** is a technique that involves dedicating specific time blocks to certain tasks or activities. This can help increase productivity and ensure you complete your most important tasks.

- **The Eisenhower Matrix** is a tool that helps you prioritize tasks based on their importance and urgency. This time management approach can help you focus on the most relevant tasks and use your time effectively.

- **The GTD (Getting Things Done)** method involves breaking down tasks into smaller, manageable steps and organizing them into categories. This approach can make you feel less overwhelmed and help increase your productivity.

Experimenting with different time management techniques can help you identify what works for you and improve your productivity and time management skills.

Prioritize your tasks

Identifying and prioritizing the most important tasks that require the most attention is important.

This can help you avoid spending too much time on less important activities and ensure that you make time for self-care.

Use a timer

Setting a timer for a specific task or activity can help you stay focused and avoid distractions.

This technique, known as the Pomodoro Technique, involves working on a task for a set amount of time and then taking a short break.

Avoid multitasking

Multitasking can lower your productivity and cause increased stress levels. It's better to focus on a single task at a time until you complete it before moving to the next one.

Here is a selection of tips on how to manage multitasking tendencies:

- When working on a task, close any unnecessary tabs or applications on your computer to minimize distractions.

- Avoid checking your email or phone frequently while working on a task. Instead, set aside a specific time to check and respond to messages.

- If you're working on a project that requires your full attention, consider putting your phone on silent or in another room to avoid interruptions.

- Use a task management system to help you stay organized and focused on one task at a time. That could be a to-do list or a project management tool.

- Do your best to eliminate any potential interruptions or distractions when working on a task. For example, go into a quiet working space free from disturbances when writing a report.

Minimize distractions

Distractions such as social media, notifications, or unnecessary phone calls can waste time and prevent you from being productive. Minimizing these distractions allows you to stay focused longer and make the most of your time.

Here are some practical tips on how to minimize distractions:

- Turn off your phone or computer notifications during work or study time to avoid distractions.

- Use apps or browser extensions that block social media or other distracting websites during certain hours or for a set amount of time.

- Set aside specific times to check and respond to emails or phone calls instead of constantly interrupting your work or leisure activities.

- Avoid multitasking, as it can lead to increased stress and decreased productivity. Instead, focus on one task at a time and complete it before moving on to the next one.

- If you work in a distracting environment, consider using noise-canceling headphones or finding a quiet workspace to help you stay focused.

Start working on these practices, one at a time.

If you have read any book from my 'Empower Yourself' series, you can remember that I emphasize the importance of taking it slow and gradual. From personal experience, I believe that's the best way to build long-lasting habits that yield the desired positive impact you need in your life.

As you work on the habits discussed above, please do your best to maintain a daily journal about them. Journaling helps you track your performance and your regularity with certain practices.

Let us forward ahead and learn about managing your finances.

Chapter 19: Managing Your Finances

"Money is only a tool. It will take you wherever you wish, but it will not replace you as the driver."
—Ayn Rand

Managing finances effectively is crucial for a comfortable and stress-free life. A budget is a useful financial planning tool that helps you track expenses, prioritize spending, and identify areas where you can make some cost savings.

A budget also enables us to allocate money towards future savings, such as an emergency fund or retirement. Saving for the future can provide a sense of security and reduce financial stress—having a safety net in place can lead to financial peace of mind.

Making informed financial decisions is equally important, especially regarding investments or loans. Conducting research and seeking advice from financial experts can help you make personal financial decisions aligned with your goals and based on accurate information.

Being aware of potential financial challenges, such as unexpected expenses or job loss, and having a readymade plan to address them can also alleviate stress and increase financial security.

On the other hand, financial mismanagement can lead to chronic financial stress that can affect mental and physical health. Financial stress causes anxiety, depression, and physical health problems such as high blood pressure and heart disease.

Seeking support from financial advisors, credit counselors, or community resources can help individuals facing financial difficulties develop a plan for debt reduction and better financial management.

Effective financial management is an essential aspect of our overall well-being.

Below are some tips to help you manage your finances effectively and ensure you empower this aspect of life too.

Create a budget

Creating a budget is the first step to managing your finances. It will help you understand your income, expenses, and savings.

- Start by listing all your income sources and then categorize your expenses.

- Keep track of your expenses to identify areas where you can cut back.

- If you're spending a lot on eating out, you can try cooking at home instead to save money.

Save for the future

Saving money is crucial to achieving long-term financial security. Start by setting savings goals and make regular contributions to your savings account.

If you're saving for a down payment on a house, save a specific amount monthly to progress towards your goal.

- Each week set a small goal to save a certain amount of money. It can be as little as $5. It is best to start small and stay consistent with saving that set amount.

- Once you get the hang of putting aside $5 every week, increase the weekly saving target.

- You can also get a good insurance policy if you are down for it.

Set savings goals

Determine how much you want to save and for what purpose. For example, you may want to save for a down payment on a house, a new car, or a vacation.

For example, if you need to save $20,000 for a down payment and want to achieve that goal in two years, you will need to save approximately $833 per month.

If you're trying to cut back on expenses to save more money, consider reducing your dining-out expenses by cooking at home more often or negotiating with service providers to get better rates.

Each year decide on something you want to save for and make it your most compelling WHY to save money.

Automate your savings

Set up automatic monthly transfers to your savings account from your checking account. This can help you stay on track with your savings goals and ensure that you're consistently contributing towards them.

Take advantage of employer benefits

Many employers offer retirement plans or 401(k) plans that provide matching contributions. Please take advantage of these benefits because they can help boost your savings.

Make informed financial decisions

Research and understand the financial products you are considering before making any decisions. Consider seeking professional advice from a financial planner if you are unsure about a decision. Before investing your money, research different investment options and consider the risks involved.

- Managing personal finances demands informed decision-making. Before making any financial decisions, research and understand the offered financial products, including the terms and conditions of credit cards, loans, or mortgages.

- Before signing up for a credit card, understand the interest rates, rewards programs, and fees involved. Similarly, before applying for a loan, understand the repayment terms, including interest rates, fees, and penalties for early repayment.

- For more complex financial decisions such as investments, seek professional advice from a financial planner. A financial planner can advise you on investment options, risks, and expected returns. They can also help you create a plan that aligns with your financial goals and risk tolerance.

- When investing money, do your due diligence, research different investment options, and consider the risks involved. For example, stocks can be volatile and carry significant risks, but they also have the potential for high returns. On the other hand, bonds are typically less risky but have lower potential returns.

Financial challenges or struggles

Recognize if you are experiencing financial difficulties, such as struggling to pay bills or accumulating debt.

Seek support and advice from a financial counselor, advisor, or a trusted friend or family member. If you're having trouble paying off debt, consider speaking to a financial counselor who can help you develop a debt management plan.

Here are some tips to help you seek support and advice:

- **Research financial counseling services in your area:** Many non-profit organizations and government agencies offer free or low-cost financial counseling services. These services can teach you to manage your finances, create a budget, and develop a debt management plan.

- **Speak to a financial advisor:** A financial advisor can help you make informed decisions about investing your money and managing your finances. They can also provide advice on retirement planning and tax strategies.

- **Seek support from a trusted friend or family member:** Talking to someone you trust about your financial situation can help you gain a new perspective and receive emotional support.

- **Consider online resources:** There are many online resources available that can help you manage your finances. For example, budgeting apps can help you track your spending and create a budget.

- **Contact your creditors:** If you are struggling to pay bills, contact your creditors and explain your situation. They may be willing to work with you to develop a payment plan or reduce your interest rate.

Track your expenses

Actively tracking your spending can help you identify areas where you can cut back and save money. Use a budgeting app or spreadsheet to track your expenses and income.

Let's say you notice that you're spending a lot of money on takeout food. Tracking your expenses can help you plan to cook more meals at home and save money on food.

Set financial goals

As mentioned, having specific financial goals can motivate you to save money and make smarter financial decisions. Whether you want to save for a down payment on a house or to pay off credit card debt, setting goals can help you stay focused on what's important.

Here are some important financial goal-setting principles you should keep in mind at all times:

- **Be specific:** Make sure your goals are clear and specific. For example, rather than setting a goal to "save money," set a goal to "save $500 a month."

- **Set a timeframe:** Give yourself a deadline to achieve your goals. Doing this will help you stay motivated and focused. For example, if you want to save $5,000 for a down payment on a car, set a timeframe of one year to achieve this goal.

- **Break it down:** Break your goal down into smaller, more manageable steps. For example, if you want to save $5,000 in one year, save $417 monthly.

- **Create a budget:** Creating a budget can help you identify areas where you can reduce spending and redirect those funds toward achieving your goals.

- **Track your progress:** Regularly monitor your progress toward your goals; it can instrumentally help you stay motivated and adjust your plan as needed.

- **Celebrate your successes:** When you achieve a financial goal, take a moment to celebrate your success. This can help keep you motivated and focused on achieving your next goal.

When you set specific financial goals, create a plan, and regularly monitor your progress, you can achieve financial security and control over your life. Remember to seek support and advice when needed and to make informed financial decisions.

Have an emergency fund

Life is always full of surprises and whether we like it or not, we need to be prepared to absorb any financial surprises that may come. For example, you or a loved one may need emergency treatment, your car could break down, the house may need some urgent repairs, you may lose your job – the list is endless!

Having money in an emergency fund ensures you can easily deal with such emergencies without having to liquidate long term investments or get into debt.

Aim to save three to six months of your living expenses in an easily accessible savings account. Let's say your car breaks down, and you must pay for a costly repair. If you have an emergency fund, you can pay for the repair without dipping into your regular savings or seeking credit.

Seek professional advice

If you are having a hard time managing your finances or need help with a specific financial issue, consider seeking advice from a financial professional such as a credit counselor or financial advisor.

You may want to consult a financial advisor who can help you create a retirement plan or invest your savings. Or, if you're struggling with debt, a credit counselor can give you actionable ideas to manage your debt and improve your credit score.

Goal setting is another important part of practical self-care. Let's talk more about how to set effective goals in the next chapter...

Chapter 20: Goal-Setting Strategies

"If you want to live a happy life, tie it to a goal, not to people or things." **—Albert Einstein**

Setting goals is a powerful way to clarify what we want to achieve and create a roadmap to get you there. Without goals, we may feel aimless or uncertain about our future, and it can be difficult to progress toward our aspirations.

On the other hand, setting goals helps us prioritize our time and energy toward the things that matter most and can provide us with a sense of accomplishment and fulfillment when we achieve them.

One of the best ways to set effective goals is to make them specific and measurable.

Vague goals such as "get healthier" or "be more productive" are difficult to achieve because they lack concrete criteria for success.

Instead, set goals like "lose 15 pounds in four months" or "write a 5,000 words for my book by the end of the month." By making our goals measurable, we can track our progress and know when we achieve success.

Breaking down our goals into smaller, manageable steps is also important because it helps prevent getting overwhelmed and makes progressing toward our larger goals easier. For example, if our goal is to run a marathon, we might break it down into small, easily achievable steps, such as running a 5K, then a 10K, and so on.

Finally, we must review and adjust our goals regularly and as needed. Life is unpredictable, and circumstances may change, so it's important to be flexible and adapt our goals accordingly. For example, after realizing that a goal is no longer relevant or attainable, we may need to revise it or set a new goal altogether.

Start with a clear vision

Before setting goals, clearly define what you want to achieve.

Take some time to reflect on your values, passions, and aspirations. Ask yourself what you want to accomplish in the short and long term.

- **Consider your personal and professional goals:** Do you want to advance in your career, improve your health, or learn a new skill? Write down your goals, and ensure you prioritize them based on their feasibility and importance.

- **Reflect on your values and passions:** What matters most to you? What do you enjoy doing? How can you incorporate your values and passions into your goals? For example, if you value creativity, you may aim to write a novel or learn to paint.

- **Visualize your ideal future:** Imagine yourself achieving your goals and living your ideal life. What does that look like? How does it feel? Use this vision to motivate and inspire you.

- **Consider potential obstacles:** What challenges might you face when working towards your goals? How can you overcome these obstacles? For example, if you're trying to save money, you may need to adjust your spending habits or find ways to increase your income.

Set specific goals

Setting specific goals helps you to stay focused and gives you a clear target. For example, instead of having a goal to "exercise more," be very specific and set something like "skip rope for 10 minutes every day."

- To set specific goals, get clarity on what you really want.

- Tune into your feelings and ask yourself, 'What do I want the most in my health, wealth, fitness, relationships, etc.?'

- It may take a while, but soon you'll start to get clear answers. When you do, write them down and focus on one goal at a time.

Make your goals achievable

Setting goals that are too difficult or unrealistic can be demotivating.

Make sure your goals are achievable and consider your current resources and abilities to achieve them by doing the following:

Break goals into smaller steps

Breaking down large goals into smaller steps that are more manageable makes them less overwhelming and helps you to stay motivated.

For example, if your goal is to write a book, break it down into chapters or sections and set a goal to write a certain number of pages each day or week.

Measure your Progress

Tracking your progress is important to stay motivated and on track. Set up a system to measure your progress, such as a spreadsheet or a journal.

- Use a fitness tracking app to log your workouts and progress towards your fitness goals.

- Keep a daily journal to track your progress on personal development goals, such as practicing gratitude or reading a certain number of pages daily.

- Use a budgeting app to track your spending and savings progress toward financial goals.

- Create a spreadsheet to track your progress on work-related goals, such as completing a project by a certain deadline or increasing sales by a certain percentage.

- Use a habit-tracking app to monitor your progress toward forming new habits, such as drinking more water or meditating daily.

Celebrate your achievements

Celebrating your achievements, no matter how small, helps to keep you motivated and encourages you to keep going. For example, treat yourself to a nice dinner or buy yourself a small gift when you reach a milestone.

Review and adjust your goals as needed

It's important to review your goals regularly and adjust them as needed. Sometimes circumstances change, and it's important to be flexible and adapt your goals accordingly.

Let's say you want to start your own business. Your first step might be researching the market and writing a business plan. Your specific goal could be to complete the business plan within one month. To make this goal achievable, you could break it down into smaller steps, such as researching the market for one week, writing the executive summary for the second week, and so on.

Use the SMART framework

SMART stands for **Specific**, **Measurable**, **Achievable**, **Relevant**, and **Time-bound.**

When setting a goal, make sure it meets these criteria. For example, instead of setting a goal like "improve my fitness,", which is vague, a SMART goal would be "skip rope for 10 minutes and achieve 500 reps within 2 months"

Here is a breakdown of the SMART framework:

- **Specific:** Be clear about what you want to achieve. Instead of saying, "learn a new skill," be specific and say, "learn how to play the guitar."

- **Measurable:** Set criteria you can use to measure your progress. For example, if your goal is to save money, set a specific amount you want to save each month.

- **Achievable:** Make sure your goal is realistic and achievable. Setting a goal that is too difficult to reach can be discouraging. For example, if you have never run before, setting a goal to run a 10K marathon in six months might not be achievable.

- **Relevant:** Always ensure all your goals are relevant to your objectives and values. For example, if you value health and fitness, setting a goal to run a 5k race might be relevant.

- **Time-bound:** Set a deadline for achieving your goal. This will help you stay focused and motivated. For example, if your goal is to save $5,000 for a down payment on a house, set a deadline of one year to achieve that goal.

Setting SMART goals ensures your goals are specific, achievable, and relevant, which gives you a clear plan for achieving them within a specific timeframe.

Write down your goals

Studies show that people who write down their goals are likelier to achieve them. Write your goals down in a notebook or on a sticky note and place it somewhere visible, such as your desk or bathroom mirror.

Share your goals with someone else

Telling a friend or family member about your goals can provide accountability and support. For example, if you want to learn a new language, tell a friend and set up regular language co-practice sessions.

Create a vision board

A vision board is a visual representation of your goals and aspirations. It can help you stay focused and motivated and remind you of what you are working toward achieving.

Set deadlines

Setting deadlines for your goals can help you stay on track and ensure you are making progress. Deadlines also create a sense of urgency, which can be motivating.

Be flexible

Being flexible and adaptable is important when working towards your goals because life is unpredictable, and circumstances change constantly. It's important to be open to adjusting your goals as needed.

- Let's assume your goal is to save $10,000 for a down payment on a house within a year. However, unforeseen circumstances, such as unexpected medical bills or car repairs, arise and make it difficult to stick to your original plan.

- Another example could be a goal to lose weight by following a specific diet and exercise plan.

- Similarly, if you set a goal to read one book per week but find that you don't have enough time due to a change in your work schedule or other commitments, you may need to adjust your goal to one book every two weeks or find ways to make time for reading in smaller increments, such as 30 minutes per day.

The key is to be open to adjusting your goals and finding creative solutions to overcome obstacles and challenges that may arise along the way.

Learn from setbacks

Setbacks are a natural part of the goal-setting process. Instead of becoming discouraged or giving up, use setbacks as an opportunity to learn and grow. Determine what went wrong and use whatever information you gather to plan and move forward.

For example, if your goal is to run a 5K. You could write it down in your planner, create a vision board with images of runners, set a deadline to complete the race by a certain date, share your goal with a friend who is also a runner, and celebrate each milestone (such as completing a 1-mile run).

Be flexible with your training schedule if you need to adjust it due to unforeseen circumstances. More importantly, learn from setbacks such as a minor injury by adjusting your training plan or seeking medical attention.

Chapter 21: Building a Supportive Environment

"Surround yourself with people who believe in your dreams, encourage your ideas, support your ambitions, and bring out the best in you."

— Roy T. Bennett

Our environment has a powerful influence on our emotional, physical, and mental health. It can impact our mood, stress and energy levels, and general well-being. Creating a supportive and positive environment can help us feel happier, healthier, and more productive.

One way to create a supportive environment is to organize and de-clutter our physical space. A cluttered and disorganized environment can lead to feelings of stress and overwhelm. Taking the time to clean up and organize our space can create a sense of calm and order, making it easier to focus and be productive.

Another important aspect of creating a supportive environment is making it comfortable and welcoming. This may involve adding personal touches like photos or artwork, choosing comfortable furniture, and incorporating elements like natural light and plants that improve our mood and well-being.

Surrounding ourselves with positive and supportive people is also important to creating a supportive environment. Positive relationships can provide a sense of belonging, emotional support, and motivation that can enhance our mental health and well-being.

De-clutter and organize

A cluttered and disorganized environment can cause stress, overwhelm, and distract us from our tasks. A great way to create a supportive environment is by de-cluttering and organizing our spaces. This means getting rid of items we no longer need or use and finding a specific place for everything else.

For example, you could:

- Go through your closet and donate clothes you haven't worn in a year

- Clear off your desk and create a filing system for papers and documents

- Tidy up your kitchen and pantry, throw away expired food, and organize items by category

By de-cluttering and organizing, you'll find what you need more easily and feel a sense of calm in your space. You'll also be less likely to misplace things or forget important tasks.

Surround yourself with positive and supportive people

The people we surround ourselves with can significantly impact our well-being.

That's why you should surround yourself with people who uplift and support you and distance yourself from those who bring negativity or stress.

Create a comfortable and welcoming space

Make your environment comfortable and welcoming using soft lighting, cozy blankets, and comfortable furniture. This can help create a sense of relaxation and comfort.

Personalize your space

Incorporate things that bring you joy and reflect your personality, such as artwork, photographs, or meaningful objects. This can help create a sense of belonging and connection to your environment.

Maintain a clean and healthy environment

A clean and healthy environment is essential for our well-being. Regularly clean and disinfect your space to promote good health.

Incorporate nature into your environment

Add some houseplants to your living space. They purify the air and provide oxygen; plants can also boost mood and reduce stress levels. Some easy-tocare-for plants include snake plants, spider plants, and pothos.

Here are some ideas on how to do this well:

- Incorporate natural materials into your decor. This could include wood furniture, stone or ceramic tiles, or natural fiber textiles like cotton or linen. These materials can add texture and warmth to a space and help to create a connection to the natural world.

- Take advantage of outdoor spaces. Spending time in nature has numerous benefits for our mental and physical health. Consider walking in a nearby park or nature preserve, or creating a small outdoor oasis in your backyard.

- Bring nature inside with artwork or photography. Consider incorporating nature-themed artwork or photographs if you can't add live plants or natural materials to your space.

- Consider the view from your windows. If you have control over your window treatments, choose options that allow natural light to enter your space and provide views of nature.

- If your view is less than inspiring, consider adding a bird feeder or potted plants outside to create a more eye-appealing scene.

Limit exposure to negative news and media

Exposure to negative news and media can negatively impact our mental and emotional well-being. News and social media platforms often focus on negative events and sensationalized stories that can increase stress and anxiety. That's why we must do our best to limit our exposure to such news to maintain our mental well-being.

Here are some tips to help you reduce your exposure to negative news:

- **Set boundaries**: Limit your time on social media platforms, TV, or radio to reduce your exposure to negative news.

- **Choose your sources wisely:** Choose sources that focus on positive and uplifting news stories instead of just sensationalized stories.

- **Take a break:** It is important to take a break from the news and social media regularly to avoid becoming overwhelmed.

- **Focus on positive news**: Consciously seek positive news stories that can uplift and motivate you.

- **Practice mindfulness:** Engage in mindfulness activities like meditation, yoga, or deep breathing exercises to help you stay centered and calm in the face of negative news.

Limiting your exposure to negative news can help reduce stress and anxiety and promote a more positive outlook.

Choose colors that promote well-being

Colors can have a powerful effect on our moods and emotions.

Here are some examples of how to incorporate colors that promote well-being:

- **Blues:** Blue is calming and serene. Consider painting a room light blue or adding blue accent pillows to a couch or bed.

- **Greens:** Green is the color of nature and can promote relaxation and rejuvenation. Adding some potted plants or a green accent wall can bring a sense of tranquility to a space.

- **Earth Tones:** Earth tones like browns and beiges can create a warm and cozy atmosphere. Consider using natural materials, such as wood or stone, in your decor.

- **Neutrals:** Neutrals like whites and grays can create a clean and minimalist look. This can promote a sense of calm and order in a space.

It's important to consider the mood and atmosphere you want to create in a space when choosing colors. Remember that colors can also affect people differently; choose colors that work for you.

Create a calming space

Having a space where you can go to relax and unwind can be incredibly beneficial for your well-being. Consider creating a cozy corner in your home with soft lighting, comfortable seating, and calming decor.

- You can put plants in the corner of your house along with a comfy chair and some books and turn it into a calming, reading corner.

- You can also turn your bedroom into your calming space by taking out the extras, including the TV and the computer, so you only focus on unwinding when you are in your room.

- You don't need anything fancy to make your calming space. Just clearing out a corner to sit and relax is sufficient.

Surround yourself with meaningful objects

Surrounding yourself with objects that have personal significance can help create a sense of connection and grounding. It can also remind you what brings you joy and fulfillment.

However, avoid hoarding or excessive clutter, which can lead to stress and overwhelm. Be selective in what you choose to display, and make sure the items are organized and well-maintained.

Here are some ideas to point you down the right path:

- Display photographs of loved ones, pets, or favorite memories in a prominent place in your home or workspace.

- Keep a memento or souvenir from a special trip or event on your desk or bedroom.

- Incorporate artwork or decorative items that reflect your personality and interests.

- Display a collection of objects you consider meaningful, such as books, vinyl records, or vintage items.

Foster positive relationships

Our relationships can have a significant impact on our well-being. Surround yourself with positive, supportive, and uplifting people. Cultivate meaningful connections with those around you.

- Start by strengthening any current relationships you would like to keep. For instance, to foster a better bond with your sister, start being deliberate about showing her more love and concern.

- Reach out to the loved ones you want to have a better bond with. Express your sentiments and tell them how much they mean to you.

- If you have strained ties with a loved one, extend a hand of love and apologize to them for being away.

- If you don't have the kind of love, friendship, and relationships your heart desires, start seeking them. For instance, if you don't have any good friends, meet more people, attend gatherings of like-minded people or even those with diverse interests, and join different social media communities. You will find a few people you will gel well with. Once you do, stay in touch with them to grow your newfound relationships.

- As for finding the love of your life, first, think about the kind of partner you want. Make a mental image of this partner and think about the traits and qualities you want in your partner. As you get more clarity on the kind of companion you want, meet more people to seek the one your heart desires. If your efforts are consistent, you will find the love of your life.

- When you start an intimate relationship, do your best to give your partner enough time, love, care, and attention and meet their needs.

- As you focus on building new, positive relationships, steer clear of the ones that add any ounce of negativity to your life. Once you distance yourself from the negative influences in life or even those who bring you down, you will automatically create more space for positive influences.

Lighting

Natural light can help regulate our circadian rhythm and improve our mood, so use natural light whenever possible.

If natural light isn't available, invest in soft, warm lighting to create a cozy and inviting atmosphere. Harsh, fluorescent lighting can cause eye strain and contribute to headaches; choose easy-on-the-eyes lighting.

Comfortable furniture

Investing in comfortable furniture can make a big difference in how you feel in your space. Choose furniture that supports good posture and encourages relaxation, such as a comfortable chair or supportive mattress. When we feel physically comfortable, it can help us feel more relaxed and focused.

Minimize distractions

Distractions can disrupt our focus and lead to stress and anxiety. Create a quiet space for work or study, and consider using noise-canceling headphones to block out distractions. We can concentrate better and feel more productive when we have a peaceful and quiet environment.

Incorporate sensory elements

Engaging your senses can help create a more enjoyable and relaxing environment. Incorporate pleasant smells, sounds, and textures in your environment, such as candles, music, or comfortable fabrics. Sensory elements can help us feel more grounded and present in our space.

Now that you know how to empower your self-care, it is time to focus on it. This guide is with you every step of the process and will push you forward towards greatness.

Conclusion

We all deserve love, care, attention, and respect. Unfortunately, we often forget that we need to treat ourselves right first. For anybody else to care for us, we need to set the benchmark properly by taking good care of ourselves first.

While self-care can seem difficult, this book has shown you that by applying simple ideas and creating a self-care routine consisting of simple but effective habits, you can empower your self-care and personal growth.

I am so proud of you for taking the time to read this book because reading it as far down as the conclusion shows you have truly begun to value yourself and are genuinely committed to empowering your self-care.

This little investment you have made by purchasing this guide is an investment in your well-being, which will continue to repay itself many times over.

As you proceed with the guide and start looking after yourself, you will notice a remarkable improvement in your mood, well-being, productivity, and every aspect of your existence and life.

Self-care is more like an elixir: it has magical effects, but only if you stick to it for the long haul, so stick to it, kindred spirit.

I wish you all the best on this beautiful journey that will make you fall in love with yourself and live a truly meaningful life.

Scott Allan

"When I loved myself enough, I began leaving whatever wasn't healthy. This meant people, jobs, my own beliefs and habits — anything that kept me small. My judgement called it disloyal. Now I see it as self-loving."

— **Kim McMillen**

About Scott Allan

Scott Allan is an international bestselling author of 25+ books published in 15 languages in personal growth and self-development. He is the author of **Fail Big**, **Undefeated,** and **Do the Hard Things First**.

As a former corporate business trainer in Japan and **Transformational Mindset Strategist**, Scott has invested over 10,000 hours of research and instructional coaching into self-mastery and leadership training.

Scott Allan is committed to a path of constant and never-ending self-improvement with an unrelenting passion for teaching, building critical life skills, and inspiring people worldwide to take charge of their lives.

Many success strategies and self-empowerment material reinventing lives worldwide evolve from Scott Allan's 20 years of practice and teaching critical skills to corporate executives, individuals, and business owners.

You can connect with Scott at:

scottallan@scottallanpublishing.com

Bonus Chapter: Empower Your Focus

Turn the page to read a chapter from **Empower Your Focus** (Book #4 in the *Pathways to Mastery* series)

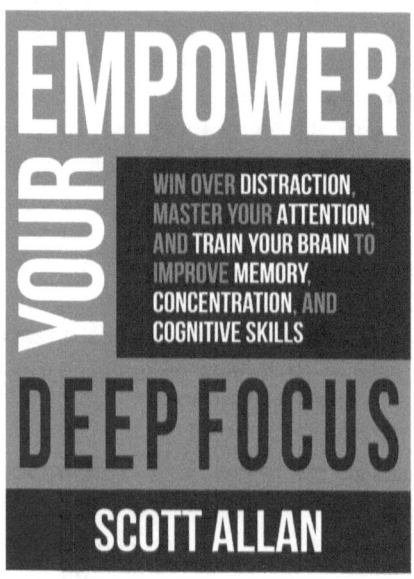

The Process of Building Focus

You've understood what focus truly is, why it matters, and how to channel the different forms of focus to your advantage. But how do you go about building focus? Where do you begin? What process do you follow, and how do you ensure your pursuit of building focus is not only fruitful but, is also sustainable and enjoyable?

The key is to begin with one thing to focus on, to complete this task or meet this goal, and then move on to your next pursuit, thus creating a continuous flow of victories, each one fueling the next. Success begets success, and the more wins you rack up, the greater confidence you will develop in your deep focus sessions.

Focus on One Thing Until Done

We've found ourselves in a world where multi-tasking is the norm and focusing on one thing at a time is an exception. However, in doing so, we sacrifice the potential for our brains to level up and cultivate the right mind with the best training.

Conditioning the mind to focus on and accomplish task after task, goal after goal, with the help of the right habits, delivers the outcome you truly desire. Instead of ending up with whatever cheap pleasure that's derived from instant gratification, you reap the benefits of a focused mind trained to execute on priority tasks.

The more we repeatedly do something, the easier it becomes to do; it becomes a pattern, a *good habit*. The scientific term for this practice is 'automaticity'. It's the ability of your mind to let you do something on autopilot. It takes a great deal of effort and time to set up a new habit.

While some studies claim it takes 21 days, others state it takes 66 days and some even say it takes 254 days for a new habit to be fully ingrained in you - but once you've managed to establish a new habit, your activity will be almost automatic. When you focus on one thing only, and one thing after another at a time, each one becomes easier to do as it becomes habitual.

Here are a few techniques which will set you on the path to building focus and sharpening your mind.

Technique 1: Create goals for yourself

It is said that the difference between a dream and a goal is that a dream is a gift you *wish to receive*, whereas a goal is an outcome you *work to achieve*. Without a concrete goal, you can't have a clear plan. Without a plan, your actions will have no particular direction, and your energies will be expended wastefully.

Here are 11 steps to help you identify, articulate, and clearly define your goals:

1. Begin with an idea dump. List out all the things you've wanted to achieve, without setting any limitations in your mind.

2. Choose your master goal. What is it that you want the most in your life? Don't winnow it down – be bold in what you're asking of yourself, and trust that you will figure out a way to make it happen. Once you've chosen your master goal, write it down and commit to it.

3. Put a timeline to your goal. It doesn't matter if it is 2 months, 2 years, or 20 years – but put a definite timeline.

4. Break down your big goal. What will you need to accomplish in the next 1 year? Reverse engineer your big goal by writing down all the steps necessary to achieve it (hence, the next step).

5. Break your big goal down into 'sub-goals'. Make a list of every task, no matter how small, and identify what it is and how much

time required to finish it. Think of this as your to-do list – what simple tasks will help you move towards accomplishing your goal?

6. Prioritize your action steps. What do you need to do right away, and what's not as urgent?

7. Visualize your success daily. Feeling how you would feel once you've accomplished your goal will fuel you to work towards it.

8. Become part of a supportive community. Invite accountability into your lifestyle. You don't have to do everything all by yourself!

9. Be mindful of your obstacles. Are you missing key resources? Do you hold limiting beliefs that are sabotaging you in your quest? Be honest and list out your obstacles so that you can find ways to overcome them.

10. Identify the skills and knowledge you need to reach your goal.

11. Continuously and honestly review your progress. Set up weekly and monthly review sessions to get an accurate benchmark of your progress.

Follow these steps and you should be well on your way to building an extraordinary level of focus.

Technique 2: Build 'focus blocks' to improve productivity

Using 'focus blocks' refers to chalking out chunks of time on your calendar for specific activities. Doing your taxes? Block out time on your calendar. Brainstorming ideas for your next project? Set aside time. Whatever task is pressing, whether it be attending your child's concert or much-required me-time, you want to dedicate time exclusively to that activity for that particular period of time.

Scheduling time is the easy part – the harder part is to ensure that you work only on that specific activity for that chunk of time, ignoring all else. This includes not checking up on interrupting emails and not pausing for a colleague dropping by for some quick help.

Here are **7 quick tips** to help you:

1. Commit to your scheduling system.

2. Use your calendar, use your stickies, use a daily planner - use every tool at your disposal to help you stick to your system.

3. Make a reasonable schedule – you don't want to burn out in the process of reaching for your optimum level of focus.

4. Get your colleagues onboard – you can share your calendar so that they can see when you're available.

5. Find a quiet and comfortable spot to work without distraction.

6. Work in sync with your natural cycle. When do you concentrate best? Set your schedule accordingly.

7. Don't give up. If you find yourself off course, gently bring yourself back to plan.

It's hard to get into the system of working with focus blocks. But, once you commit to it—and discuss it with your colleagues—you can request that they not interrupt, and you'll find a tremendous boost in productivity.

Technique 3: Use focus-building activities in a group setting

While the first two techniques were inward-focused, here's another technique to help you start building better focus, and this one can be group-based. Pick a focus-building activity, and schedule time with friends or family centered around this activity. Think 'puzzle-night'!

You probably worked on a lot of puzzles as a child —puzzles are a great way to stimulate the mind and build focus not only in children, but also in adults.

Here are **five benefits** of using puzzles as a work-out for your brain:

1. Improve cognitive function and spatial reasoning

2. Develop better attention to detail

3. Improve your memory, especially short-term memory

4. Enhance your problem-solving ability and IQ over time

5. Immerse yourself in an esteem-boosting activity and reduce stress

If jigsaw puzzles aren't your thing, you can go with crossword games, solve brain teasers, work with Sudoku, or even use apps such as Luminosity. If you're a chess player, it can be a fantastic way improve focus as well.

No matter which technique you choose to begin your journey of improving your ability to focus, you want to ensure you commit to one thing at a time and stay on course.

The process of building focus is an ongoing challenge, but it comes with life-changing rewards that make it totally worth the commitment.

About Scott Allan

Scott Allan is an international bestselling author of over 30 books published in 12 languages in the area of personal growth and self-development. He is the author of **Fail Big**, **Undefeated,** and **Do the Hard Things First**.

As a former corporate business trainer in Japan, and **Transformational Mindset Strategist**, Scott has invested over 10,000 hours of research and instructional coaching into the areas of self-mastery and leadership training.

With an unrelenting passion for teaching, building critical life skills, and inspiring people around the world to take charge of their lives, Scott Allan is committed to a path of **constant and never-ending self-improvement**.

Many of the success strategies and self-empowerment material that is reinventing lives around the world evolves from Scott Allan's 20 years of practice and teaching critical skills to corporate executives, individuals, and business owners.

You can connect with Scott at:

scottallan@scottallanpublishing.com

www.scottallanpublishing.com

www.scottallanbooks.com

Scott Allan

"Master Your Life One Book at a Time."

<u>Subscribe</u> to the weekly newsletter for actionable content and updates on future book releases from Scott Allan